EVERYDAY CROCHET

Wearable Designs Just for You

DORIS CHAN

TECHNICAL EDITOR &
ILLUSTRATOR KAREN MANTHEY

POTTER
CRAFT

NEW YORK

Published in the United States by Potter Craft, an imprint of
the Crown Publishing Group, a division of Random House, Inc.,
New York.
www.crownpublishing.com
www.pottercraft.com

POTTER CRAFT and CLARKSON N. POTTER are trademarks,
and POTTER and colophon are registered trademarks of
Random House, Inc.

Library of Congress Cataloging-in-Publication Data

Chan, Doris.
  Everyday crochet / Doris Chan ; technical editor and illustrator
Karen Manthey.—1st ed.
    p. cm.
 1. Crocheting—Patterns. I. Manthey, Karen. II. Title.
  TT820.C44 2007
   746.43'4041—dc22

                        2007000245

ISBN 978-0-307-35373-3

Printed in China

Design by Laura Palese
Technical editing and illustrations by Karen Manthey

10 9 8 7 6 5 4 3 2 1

First Edition

Dedication

This book is dedicated to my father, Kai Ham Chan, in loving memory. From my dad I learned, among other things, these very important Lessons of Life: (1) how to eat, (2) how to work, (3) how to knot a half-Windsor tie, (4) the difference between a safety and a touchback, and (5) the customer is always right, and even if he isn't right you should still make damn sure that he walks away absolutely convinced that he is.

acknowledgments

Hi Mom, hi Harry, hi Nick. Is this a déjà vu, or what?

Doing a second book was like handling a burlap bag full of bobcats. To my utter amazement I survived unscathed, save for a few missing patches of hair.

Karen Manthey, my tech editor, deserves most of the credit for taming the cats. Okay, she deserves *all* the credit. For the language of crochet, Karen is the planet's most skilled interpreter.

John, partner in life and life preserver, gets major points for suggesting that I sleep once in while and for keeping me from starving. We are living proof that one can live on cheesesteaks alone.

Love to the The Musketeers—Vashti Braha, Tammy Hildebrand, Marty Miller, and Diane Moyer—who continue to serve as my cheering section, Greek chorus, and support group. Having infiltrated the upper echelons of the CGOA, we now set our sights on . . . the world. Pretty soon everyone will want to be a Musketeer, mark my words.

Hugs to the trio of Lerro women who unknowingly helped me in my quest for better-fitting crochet garments by wearing all those Christmas and birthday gifts: Lorraine, my other mom, and Anne and Cameo, my earliest models.

My thanks to all the ladies who, two years ago, answered my call for extra-sizing info and entrusted to me the secrets of their crochet desires—and their measurements!

I express the joy of being a member of the Crochet Guild of America. The annual Chain Link conferences provide treasured opportunities to commune with others who speak crochet (see Musketeers above). Hardly anything else could get me on a plane.

My thanks to these yarn contacts for so generously and unstintingly supplying materials for this book: Susan Haviland, Nancy Gadue, Angela Mantele, Jonelle Raffino, Uyvonne Bigham, Norah Gaughan, Judy Croucher, Matt Mole, Ivy Strausberg, Jeffrey Denecke, Kathy Muhr, and Margrit and Marie of Morehouse Farm.

For their enthusiastic and unwavering support of my design career and the checks, I wish to thank: Nancy Thomas (Tahki/Stacy Charles), Cari Clement (Caron International), Pam Allen, Judy Swartz and Marilyn Murphy (Interweave), Carol Alexander (DRG), Brett Bara and Adina Klein (Soho), Valerie Kurita (Meredith).

And the Potter Craft team gets full marks for making it all possible: editors Rosy Ngo, Erin Slonaker, Christina Schoen, Stephanie Klose, designer Laura Palese, publicist Ava Kavyani, and the big kahuna, Jenny Frost.

And, finally, my thanks to Cookie, the fat white Chihuahua, for keeping my work area tidy by absconding with any ball band or stitch marker that hits the floor.

contents

introduction

Did you ever take that battery of aptitude tests? Did well at spatial relations? (If you fold up this flat shape, which solid shape does it make? Or if you pull this lever, what happens?) Did you pay attention in basic geometry? Ever make a Venn diagram? Ever beat Tetris?

The ability to do mental gymnastics is way useful in crochet. With me it's an unconscious thing, intuitive, a way of looking at stuff outside the box. When you take a set of written instructions, guided only by two-dimensional diagrams and schematics, and translate them into three-dimensional crochet, you do spatial relations, geometry, logic, planning, and strategy along with the physical act of making stitches. Crocheters are smart; crochet makes us smarter.

Hear me out on this before you consign me to the funny farm. I am convinced that crochet transcends the three dimensional and enters an extra dimension I will call the Cth dimension. It's the Zen of crochet—the gestalt of crochet. If you encompass all the elements of thought, emotion, experience, and the physical acts that go into crocheting a garment and consider them as a whole, that garment amounts to more than the sum of its parts. It's not just a sweater; it's the excitement of choosing that yarn, the tactile pleasure of handling yarn and hook, the mind-numbing comfort of making the stitches, the agony of having to rip out the yoke four times because you got lost when your markers fell out, the thrill of pride when you block the piece and it comes out exactly to your measurements. Every time I wear a garment I have crocheted, it isn't merely the three-dimensional that I wear, but the Cth dimension as well.

You see, I absolutely love wearing stuff I've crocheted. I try to do it every day. Call it pride or hubris; call me an incorrigible show-off. It makes me happy. But, alas, I am not a standard size. It's been hell finding crochet patterns for garments I liked. Once found, those patterns often needed major surgery in order to look good on me. That's one of the reasons I began designing my own garments.

If you would love to wear your own creations, but struggle with the crocheting because you have fitting or sizing issues, then dive in here. From sleek camisoles to pullovers, cardigans, and coats, the designs in this book contain the elements and guidance to help you make well-fitting, attractive crocheted clothes that you will be proud to wear.

A crocheter recently commented that my designs were challenging, but not impossible. That will be my epitaph. So I ask you to please read over these next few pages of information, techniques, and warnings before you begin. My dearest wish is that you have a successful and satisfying experience with these designs so every day you, too, can walk around positively *glowing* in the Cth dimension.

|1|
EVERYDAY
GARMENTS

Made it? Flaunt it! Crocheted clothes are not just for special occasions. If you crochet, then you can make garments to wear every day using the yarns you love. "Who would want to?" you ask. Well, think about it. You can't deny there's a great deal of pride and satisfaction in crocheting something, anything. To some extent we all seek the admiration, approval, and dumbstruck awe that skillfully crocheted objects inspire. But how many admirers can there be for pretty afghans and decorative items that stay at home? Or for those gorgeous but frivolous accessories you adore wearing, but that only come out during the holidays?

I see many possible reasons for not putting your yarn stash on your back more often. Never crocheted a garment before? We will fix that. Haven't met the right crochet design? Maybe we can fix that. Can't find patterns in your size? Ditto. Think you can't wear or don't look good in crochet? It's not *you*, it's the crocheted garment that's either too clunky and thick, isn't your size, or has no shape. We can fix that, too. Aren't sure how to mix crochet with your own clothes? I can't give you a makeover, but I hope the photos of crochet plus wardrobe staples will give you some ideas.

EXTRA SIZING SPOKEN HERE

Nobody, *no body* is perfect. To be human—especially to be a human woman—is to have bulges. From birth we are told that some bulges are sexy and desirable, worthy of flaunting, while some other bulges are unsightly, best kept disguised. Who made those rules? How are we supposed to maintain any kind of self-esteem when our fashion icons are size 4 and the average American woman is size 14?

I am ashamed to admit that I totally bought into this worship of the slender. Until very recently I hadn't even considered sizing my designs larger than XL, with a finished bust around 44" (112cm). And for the most part, the editors and publishers for whom I designed were not much concerned about it. Today I am acutely aware of the need for good crochet design for other than tiny model figures. But, be assured, this book isn't for large sizes only. Every garment here is offered from small (to fit busts sized 32–34" [81–84cm]) through extra sizing (to fit busts up to 50" [127cm]), and some larger still. Many designs are Petite-able and Tall-able. If we aren't encouraged to rejoice in our various bulges, at least we can dress them in crochet.

This book is about options. Each of the following design chapters offers a basic clothing item, then runs through a gang of variations on the theme. Your perfect sweater probably won't be like any of the samples I have crocheted, because you are going to shop for the bits to do for yourself, sort of one from column A, one from column B. Add up the parts you want for the silhouette that works best for your body, whatever your size.

THE DREADED RAGLAN

Understand that I design garments from the neck down with raglan-type increases in pattern to shape the shoulders and arms. Many readers will appreciate my MO for the technical crochet aspects but will immediately dismiss the thought of raglans as intrinsically unattractive. And normally that'd be correct. Most real figures will look best in a shoulder that's more structured, with a defined shoulder line and set-in sleeves. But in order to hang properly and look good, structured garments require precise calculation of various slopes, perfect placement of the shoulder seam, *and* skillful seaming.

I never enjoyed crocheting garments this way because of the sewing. It's not that I dislike or disapprove of sewing or seaming in crochet; it's more that I've always been so lousy at it. And as for sewn raglan seams in crochet, they're the most horrible, unyielding, bulky, constricting, and restricting style imaginable. *This* raglan's different. This raglan is a gentle, almost invisible (or very pretty where perceptible) line of increasing stitch pattern. It creates a smooth, flexible, shapely shoulder that allows the fabric to stretch, drape, and mold to the wearer in ways a more structured garment could never hope to do.

Of course, there's no guarantee that it will look good on everyone. But I know for a fact that it is flattering on many who have worn my garments, and I hope you will at least give it a try.

WHAT'S UP WITH ALL THE SHELLS?

Crocheted shells possess many unique qualities. The nature of a shell, consisting of multiple tall stitches all made in one spot, is that it wants to expand. I exploit this tendency by crocheting shell fabric from the top down. If allowed, the shells across any row tend toward maximum entropy by spilling out horizontally. Normally, each successive row or round of shell stitch pattern keeps this tendency in check, resulting in a straight, in-line piece of fabric.

However, if crocheted in a relaxed enough gauge, that room for expansion is always present—lurking. So, for instance, the shell may stay quietly in place, flat and perfect, going down the middle of the back. It may stretch out long and lean at the waistline, at the middle of your sleeve, or at the diagonal of a raglan shaping. Or it may give up its full potential for width around the top of the arm, across the bust and hip. Left unchecked, shells will make beautiful flares at the lower edges of your garment. Without much ado, you're creating a gentle bell at the bottom of your sleeve, a bit of room over the top of your hip where your sweater stops, and a bit of an A-line at the hem of your skirt or dress. This self-molding aspect of shells cannot truly manifest when you work from the bottom up.

Shaping shells is at times complex. There are the problems of how to fit them in, how to pick the pattern back up when the work has changed, and how to achieve the most elegant shaping within the amount of space available. Agonizingly, there is no magic formula—no brilliant algorithm that will give you the perfect number of increases and rows for every application. The more you mess around with your own pattern shaping, the more you come to realize how much variation there can be from stitch pattern to stitch pattern, from yarn to yarn, even from a yarn worked firmly to the same yarn worked loosely. No worries! Enabled by years of trial and error and a tiny bit of math, I have crunched the numbers for the designs in this book. Once you get the hang of increasing one flavor of shell, you should find shaping the shell variation in the next project much easier.

SUBSTITUTING YARNS? JUST DO IT

Criticism of crocheted garments stems from outdated perceptions. It is true that once upon a time we were offered only pot holder fabric to wear—heavy, lifeless synthetic yarns worked with undersized hooks into clunky, frumpy garments. It is still assumed crocheters do not, will not, or cannot work with good yarns or luxury fibers, even when we can afford the cost. I was shocked and dismayed in a local yarn shop when I overheard a customer inquiring if she could crochet with a particularly lovely yarn labeled for knitting and being told no.

That customer should have been assured that any yarn that can be knitted can be crocheted. *Anything* you can wrap around your hook can be crocheted, including string, fabric, trash bags, wire, fishing line, or Twizzlers (don't ask!). Modern science has removed the stigma from synthetics. There are high-quality polyester and acrylic microfibers available. In a blend, microfiber adds strength, durability, softness, and sheen and takes away excess weight. The trendiest new yarns come from the fields, made from bamboo, soy, corn, and Tencel (derived from trees). The fineness, hand, and color properties of these alternative fibers rival those of silk, and can be found at a fraction of the cost.

Personally, I love messing with all kinds of yarns and fibers. I have my favorites as, I imagine, do you. For the purposes of this book I restricted the texture, color, and weight range of the yarns. I chose mostly smooth or slightly textured yarns so that the stitch patterns and the shape of the garments would come through. To keep the largest size garments from weighing a ton, I went no thicker than medium to heavy worsted weight, leaving the bulky and super-bulky yarns for belts.

Each of the design chapters begins with a Yarn Note that gives general guidelines for the most appropriate yarn weights. Then, for each pattern, I list the specific yarn and amounts used. I encourage you to substitute your favorite yarn or combination of yarns and colors. You want it in black? Make it in black. As long as you can achieve the stated gauge, switching hooks if needed, *just do it.*

If you're an adventurous soul and are willing to live with the results, you can break the strict gauge rule. I gauged up (used a larger hook and thicker yarn) on purpose to turn a pullover design into a heavier coat and loved it so much I put it in this book (see Shannon, page 116). But for the most part, try to stay close to the given gauge for each design, because when you stray too far, the proportions start to get hinky.

How do you know if your favorite yarn is the right weight? Annoyingly, not all yarns are labeled with either the CYCA standard ball band symbols (see Abbreviations and Symbols, page 140) or any hint at crochet gauge. If the label on the yarn you want to use is naked, it is possible to interpret the knitting gauge, which mysteriously enough most labels seem to have, and match that to a ball band symbol on the CYCA chart for the yarn weight. I may refer to knitting gauges when talking about what yarns are right for what designs as a further aid in identifying appropriate yarn weights.

To estimate how much of your choice of yarn you will need, look at the yarn listing info for a specific sample, and multiply the yardage by the number of balls or hanks needed. That's approximately how many yards it takes. Have on hand that many yards of your yarn, with extra for insurance, especially if you want to lengthen or alter.

Bear in mind that when you swap out yarns there may be unexpected consequences. There's no way I can predict for you how your yarn will react, finish, and block when it's done. The biggest glitch will be length. Often you can match the stitch gauge but not the row gauge. You can still make the pattern, but be prepared to adjust the length. Some of the other proportions may be affected, but not to the point where your results become unwearable.

HAVE A FIT

The most significant decision you will make is which pattern size to crochet, and for that you have to know yourself. It might seem as if choosing your size would be a simple matter. Unfortunately, this is never the case. My patterns do not conform to standard sweater sizes, such as S, M, L, or XL, or to American dress sizes such as 8, 10, 12, or 14. I use instead the finished garment bust measurement as the size. Due to the difference in stitch pattern width, the sizes may jump by as little as two inches (5cm) and as many as five inches (12.5cm) to the next size. How do you choose the right size? Each design chapter begins with a Size Finder, but here are general guidelines:

Measure your bust around the fullest part, wearing the bra you'd wear with the garment, one that fits properly. If you feel the crochet stitches in my designs are too open and revealing to wear over just a bra, then invest in camisoles with honest support—a built-in real bra, not the ones with bits of elastic called a shelf bra.

Next, focus on how you like your clothes to fit. Take out your favorite sweater and measure it. If you wear your sweaters small and snug, your size will be close to or smaller than your actual bust measurement. Want an oversized vest to layer over a sweatshirt? Choose the size that is your bust measurement plus a few inches of ease.

Begin with a design that is appropriate for your figure. My clothes are meant to be relaxed, made without much fussy fitting, but that does not mean they are all boxy or have no shape. I wish you could see and handle the fabric of each sample to realize how beautifully it will drape on the body. The piece should skim over your curves, taking its shape from your own. Note that I don't offer any waist shaping in these designs. If you want to emphasize a tiny waist, or suggest a waist where there is none, try belting a longer cami or pullover top or place a closure at the waist of an open-front style to nip it in.

Read the instructions, paying particular attention to any adjustment points. You are responsible for making these adjustments (or not) for your figure. The following will be most common.

Bust Short Rows: This adjustment adds a bit of fabric length to cover your bust while leaving the overall bust measurement the same. You know why we do this if you are constantly tugging at your top to keep it down in front. Most designs here offer this interior shaping, placed 1½–2½" (3.8–5cm) lower than the joining at underarms, 1–2"(2.5–5cm) in from the center at each side. This adjustment might not be enough for truly ample bust lines (bra cup sizes larger than DD). Your best option would be to size up.

Hip Shaping: Many women have told me that they could wear a size 14, but because of their hips they have to go up to a 16. It may not be an issue with shorter tops that end above the widest part of the hip, but for longer styles, if your hips are larger than the size you want to make for your bust measurement, consider doing hip shaping where offered. Also try side vents for added ease.

Sleeve Width: Due to the limitations imposed by the stitch patterns, the sleeves jump in width, with the smallest size being a bit tighter and the largest sizes looser than standard. So even when the design calls for a full-width sleeve, made straight down the length of the arm, I suggest tapering the upper arm in the largest sizes for a neater appearance and less bulk. See specific instructions for each design.

Sleeve Length: Shorten or lengthen the sleeve at the adjustment point. Feel free to make your sleeves whatever length you like—short, half, three-quarter, full-length—on any of the designs with sleeves. The raglan construction makes a yoke with a slightly capped shoulder, so any sleeveless option is actually a tiny cap sleeve. You can turn any style sleeveless by working only the first round of sleeve and ending there. My only suggestion is to not end a short sleeve right at the widest part of your bust.

Body Length: Lengthen or shorten the body at this adjustment point, usually at the very end or just before any finishing or trim. Feel free to make any top into a tunic. My suggestion? End your top either *above* or *below* the widest part of your body.

A truly wonderful aspect of neck-down construction is that you can try on your piece and check the fit as you go without much fuss. A great checkpoint is once you get the underarms joined and have worked the couple of rounds up to the bust short-row option. Keep in mind this will not be an orderly fit; the neckline might be sloppy because it needs the finishing to bring it under control, and the armholes might feel high. Blocking will normally draw out the raglan shaping and true the armhole depth. Try your garment on occasionally as you are working to get a general idea of how low to go. Remember, many yarns and stitches will grow in length with the weight of the rest of the garment, so don't be tempted to add length unless you mean it.

Some of these designs have no extra finishing at the lower body and sleeves. They just end with pattern. This is deliberate and not the lazy way out! I find this lower edge of shells quite pretty and finished-looking as is, but more than a design element, this is a calculated fitting ploy. Let's say you've blocked your sweater and discover to your horror that you've made gorilla arms. Since the bottom edge is stitch pattern, simply undo the tail end, rip as much as you want, then reweave the end. I'll tell you, this has saved my butt more times than I like to admit.

I TOLD YOU SO

Don't make me say I told you so! Before you begin, check out these standard operating procedures for all garments.

Basic supplies are needed but not listed each time, including split-ring markers or scraps of contrasting yarn for markers, scissors, tape measure, and a yarn needle in the appropriate size for weaving ends and sewing seams.

Please don't freak out at the length and seeming complexity of the patterns. In order to write instructions for so many sizes (from six sizes to as many as ten!) there had to be many more words than in your average crochet pattern. Read through, highlight, or otherwise mark the specific instructions for your size, and you'll find that it isn't that daunting after all.

Crochet to the stated gauge. Most of the time this should be rather relaxed, with the hook gliding in and out of the stitches easily. (If you find you can only hit the gauge by working so tightly that you have to struggle to insert the hook, your yarn is probably too thick for the design.) The exceptions are the belts, which are crocheted firmly, and certain finishing steps, where you need to control the neck, front, or sleeve edges. I will always tell you when you are expected to crochet to a tighter gauge. Switch to a smaller hook if needed.

With the exception of the cami-tanks, assume a basic description for all garments is "crocheted from the neck down with raglan-type increases in pattern at four 'corners' to shape the shoulders."

Directions are given for smallest size. Changes for other sizes are in parentheses.

Mark your corners and all other checkpoints as directed. Move the corner markers and don't let them fall out, or you will suffer tremendous aggravation and much ripping. I mention split-ring markers, but use anything you like. To wrap yarn markers up as you go, start with a good length of yarn, and flip it back and forth through the corner stitch as you work it, so it stays woven into the increase line.

Every garment here uses the BASE CH/SC for the foundation (see Glossary, page 138).

Weave in the loose ends. I like to thread the yarn ends on a needle and run them down and back up through a tall stitch.

Block to measurements. This is not necessary for belts, but for garments, use whatever blocking method you prefer. I always wet-block everything, removing excess moisture in the spin cycle of my washer or by rolling the work in towels. Then lay the garment flat, ease it gently into shape, and allow it to dry completely. Some yarns will stretch out of shape when wet, while others will seize and shrink. When dry, most will resume correct proportions as calculated in the schematics. If you swap yarns or alter length, expect to compensate accordingly.

2
SLEEK STARTERS
CAMI-TANKS

Getting dressed is always a matter of adequate coverage. This basic design, featuring a modest neckline, snug fit at the underarms, and wide straps, is bra-friendly and manages to cover some of the bulgy underarm bits (if you've got them). It's done in a pretty shell stitch with plenty of stretch that is a bit open but not see-through. The barer Cameo (page 18) morphs into a full-coverage Sweet Tea (page 24) by simply crocheting more around the armholes and neck. A longer A-line tunic, Somnambulista (page 26), has added shaping at the waist and hip. Crocheted in smooth, lightweight yarn, the result is a sleek starting layer you'll often reach for to wear under crocheted tops, cardigans, and jackets; under your favorite shirts and tops; or by itself when the situation calls.

YARN NOTES

The yarns used in the samples range from sportweight to light DK, ball band symbols 2 and 3. The knitting gauge is between 5 and 6 stitches per inch (2.5cm). They each behave differently, but will all give satisfactory results when crocheted to gauge.

SIZE FINDER

As a first layer, these cami-tanks are designed to fit very closely, with optional front short rows that allow more breathing room for the bust. Because the fit needs to be so intimate, I offer all the possible sizes, even though they don't exactly correspond to standard clothing sizes. Choose a size smaller than your actual bust measurement, closer to your chest measurement taken up under your arms. This could be 2, 3, or even 4" (2.5, 7.5, or 10cm) smaller than your bust, depending on how form-fitting you want your cami-tank to be. Keep in mind that this fabric is stretchy.

To wear as a vest or roomier nightgown or if your hips are more than 3" (7.5cm) larger than your bust, I suggest you size up. Choose the size closest to but not larger than your actual bust measurement. It is not always necessary to make all the adjustments for length. You must decide for your figure if and where you need more or less length, strap, torso, or skirt.

CAMEO

The front and back of this camisole are equally scooped out, which makes it simple to crochet. In this dressy, silvery wool yarn, it's a lovely everyday layer peeking out from under a blazer or jacket and sensational, if minimal, on its own for evening. Swap out the yarn for something cottony or casual to make a warm-weather top.

CAMEO

Skill Level	INTERMEDIATE	3 LIGHT

Size

Finished bust: 30 (32, 35, 37, 40, 42, 45, 47, 50, 52)" (76 [81, 88, 94, 101.5, 106.5, 114, 119, 127, 132]cm)

Materials

Filatura Di Crosa Sera; 84% wool, 11% viscose, 5% polyamide; 1¾ oz (50g)/147 yd (135m)

3 (4, 4, 5, 5, 6, 6, 6, 7, 7) balls in #40 (silver)

Size G-7 (4.5mm) crochet hook

Size G-6 (4mm) crochet hook for finishing

Gauge

Using larger hook, 13 BASE CH/SC = 4" (10cm)

In shell pattern, 2 repeats = 2½" (6.5cm); 6 rows = 2½" (6.5cm), unstretched

Using smaller hook, 14 sc = 4" (10cm)

INSTRUCTIONS

This tank is made from the neck down, with identical front and back worked separately to the underarm, then joined for the body. Make the optional minimum or maximum short rows for a full bust or if you choose a size that is seriously tight-fitting for your actual bust. Straps are worked in one while finishing.

Note: Use larger hook throughout. Smaller hook is used for finishing rounds of strap and neckline only.

FIRST FRONT/BACK

BASE CH/SC 29 (29, 29, 33, 33, 37, 37, 37, 37, 37) to measure approximately 9 (9, 9, 10, 10, 11, 11, 11, 11, 11)" (23 [23, 23, 25.5, 25.5, 28, 28, 28, 28]cm) slightly stretched. Set up 7 (7, 7, 8, 8, 9, 9, 9, 10, 10) pattern repeats as follows:

Sizes 30 (32, 35, 37, 30, 42, 45, 47)
Foundation Row: Ch 1, sc in first sc, [sk next sc, SH in next sc, sk next sc, sc in next sc] 7 (7, 7, 8, 8, 9, 9, 9) times, placing sc in last sc, turn—7 (7, 7, 8, 8, 9, 9, 9) pattern repeats (shells).
Work PATT ROW 2, PATT ROW 1 for 1 (2, 3, 3, 3, 3, 4, 4) times, PATT ROWS 3–4, PATT ROWS 2–3. Fasten off—10 (11, 12, 13, 13, 14, 15, 15) pattern repeats.

Sizes 50 (52)
Foundation Row: Ch 4, (dc, ch 1, dc) in first sc, [sk next

Special Stitches

SH: (Dc, ch 1, dc, ch 1, dc) in same stitch or space

INC-SH: [Dc, (ch 1, dc) 4 times] in same stitch or space

INC SHELL

TSH (trim shell): (2 dc, ch 2, 2 dc) in same stitch or space

Stitch Pattern Notes

This is a pattern of staggered open shells separated by sc.

STITCH PATTERN (IN ROWS, FOR FRONT/BACK)

To increase at each end following an increase row:

PATT ROW 1: Ch 4, (dc, ch 1, dc) in first dc, sc in next dc, [SH in next sc, sc in second dc of next sh] across, placing sc in second dc of last sh, SH in third ch of tch, turn.

To increase at each end following an even row:

PATT ROW 2: Ch 4 (counts as dc, ch 1), (dc, ch 1, dc) in first sc, [sc in second dc of next sh, SH in next sc] across, placing SH in last sc, turn.

To work even after an increase row:

PATT ROW 3: Ch 4 (counts as dc, ch 1), dc in first dc, sc in next dc, [SH in next sc, sc in second dc of next SH] across, placing sc

in second dc of last sh, (dc, ch 1, dc) in third ch of tch, turn.

PATT ROW 4: Ch 1, sc in first dc, [SH in next sc, sc in second dc of next SH] across, placing last sc in third ch of tch, turn.

BASIC SHELL PATTERN IN ROWS

STITCH PATTERN (IN ROUNDS, FOR BODY)

PATT RND 1: Ch 3, [sc in second dc of next sh, SH in next sc] to end, except omit last SH, instead end with (dc, ch 1, dc) in same sc as beg, sc in top of tch, turn.

PATT RND 2: Ch 1, sc in next dc, [SH in next sc, sc in second dc of next sh] to end, except omit last sc, instead end with sl st in beg sc, turn.

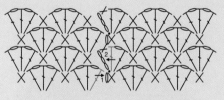

BASIC SHELL PATTERN IN ROUNDS

sc, sc in next sc, sk next sc, SH in next sc] 9 times, placing SH in last sc, turn—10 (10) pattern repeats. Work PATT ROW 1 for 5 (6) times, PATT ROWS 3–4, PATT ROWS 2–3. Fasten off—16 (17) pattern repeats.

SECOND FRONT/BACK

Make same as First Front/Back. Do not fasten off.

JOINING

Turn both pieces and join with additional stitches at underarms as follows.

All Sizes Join Row: Ch 1, sc in first dc, *work in pattern across piece, placing last sc in third ch of tch, ch 1, BASE CH/SC 7 (7, 7, 7, 11, 11, 11, 15, 15, 15) for underarm*, sc in first dc of other piece, repeat from * to * across piece and other underarm, sl st in beg sc, fasten off.

BODY

Turn and begin to work back and forth in joined

rounds. Move seam to center of underarm by skipping first 3 (3, 3, 3, 5, 5, 5, 7, 7, 7) sc of underarm base ch/sc, join with sl st in next sc.

Sizes 30 (32, 35, 37)

Rnd 1: Ch 3, *sk next sc of underarm, sc in next sc, sk remaining sc of underarm, [SH in next sc, sc in second dc of next sh] 11 (12, 13, 14) times, SH in next sc, sk first sc of underarm, sc in next sc, sk next sc*, SH in next sc; repeat from * to *, end with (dc, ch 1, dc) in same sc as beg, sc in top of beg ch, turn—24 (26, 28, 30) pattern repeats.

Sizes 40 (42, 45)

Rnd 1: Ch 1, sc in same sc, *sk next sc of underarm, SH in next sc, sk next sc, sc in next sc, sk remaining sc of underarm, [SH in next sc, sc in second dc of next sh] 14 (15, 16) times, SH in next sc, sk first sc of underarm, sc in next sc, sk next sc, SH in next sc, sk next sc*, sc in next sc; repeat from * to *, end with sl st in beg sc, turn—32 (34, 36) pattern repeats.

Sizes 47 (50, 52)

Rnd 1: Ch 3, *sk next sc of underarm, sc in next sc, sk next sc, SH in next sc, sk next sc, sc in next sc, sk remaining sc of underarm, [SH in next sc, sc in second dc of next sh] 16 (17, 18) times, SH in next sc, sk first sc of underarm, sc in next sc, sk next sc, SH in next sc, sk next sc, sc in next sc, sk next sc*, SH in next sc; repeat from * to *, end with (dc, ch 1, dc) in same sc as beg, sc in top of beg ch, turn—38 (40, 42) pattern repeats.

To get everyone on the same page, Sizes 40, 42, and 45 need this next extra round.

Sizes 40 (42, 45)

Work PATT RND 1.

All Sizes

Rnd 2: Work PATT RND 2.

Now all sizes are on the same page. You just completed the sc at the center of the right underarm, RS now facing, with work moving toward the Front. If not making short rows, skip to Rnd 3 below.

Minimum adjust for full bust

Row A (RS): Put the loop on the hook on hold. Sk next 1 (1, 1, 1, 1, 1, 1, 2, 2, 2) shells, join new yarn with sl st in second dc of next sh, [SH in next sc, sc in second dc of next sh] 9 (10, 11, 12, 13, 14, 5, 14, 15, 16) times, except omit last sc, instead sl st in second dc of next sh, turn—9 (10, 11, 12, 13, 14, 15, 14, 15, 16) pattern repeats.

Row B (WS): Sl st in dc, ch-sp and dc of first sh, [SH in next sc, sc in second dc of next sh] 8 (9, 10, 11, 12, 14, 13, 14, 15) times, except omit last sc, instead sl st in second dc of next sh, turn—8 (9, 10, 11, 12, 14, 13, 14, 15) pattern repeats, fasten off. Put the loop that is on hold back on the hook, then continue with the Body.

Note: If you made A and B short rows, ignore the sl sts and work the next round in pattern as facing.

Rnd 3 (RS): Work PATT RND 1.

Maximum adjust for fullest bust

You just completed a shell at the center of the right underarm. Put the loop on the hook on hold, turn. WS now facing, skip back to other underarm, and work as follows across the Front.

Row C (WS): Sk sh at center of left underarm, sk next 0 (0, 0, 0, 0, 0, 0, 1, 1, 1) shells, join new yarn with sl st in second dc of next sh, [SH in next sc, sc in second dc of next sh] 10 (11, 12, 13, 14, 15, 16, 15, 16, 17) times, except omit last sc, instead sl st in second dc of next sh, turn—10 (11, 12, 13, 14, 15, 16, 15, 16, 17) pattern repeats.

Row D (RS): Sl st in dc, ch-1 sp, and dc of first sh, then [SH in next sc, sc in second dc of next sh] 9 (10, 11, 12, 13, 14, 15, 14, 15, 16) times, except omit last sc, instead sl st in second dc of next sh, turn—9 (10, 11, 12, 13, 14, 15, 14, 15, 16) shells, fasten off. Put loop on hold back on the hook, continue with Body. **Stop here for Somnambulista, continued on page 28.**

BODY CONTINUED

Note: If you made C and D short rows, ignore the sl sts and work the next round in pattern as facing. Beginning by working PATT RND 2, work even on 24 (26, 28, 30, 32, 34, 36, 38, 40, 42) pattern repeats for 27 (27, 27, 27, 25, 25, 25, 29, 29, 29) more rounds, ending with PATT RND 2 for high hip length.

Adjusting body length

For Petite, omit 2 rounds (approximately 1" [2.5cm]) or more to desired length. For Tall, add 2 rounds (approximately 1" [2.5cm]) or more to desired length.

FINISHING

This version features narrow 1" (2.5cm) straps, with 3 rounds sc at the armhole and 3 rounds sc at the neck. Any less strap results in too little structure and an insecure feeling. Straps are worked as one with armhole finishing.

Adjusting Strap length

For Petite or high armholes, omit 2 BASE CH/SC (approximately ½" [1.75cm]) when making Strap, and reduce number of sc around armholes accordingly. For Tall or deep armholes, add 2 BASE CH/SC (approximately ½" [1.75cm]) when making Strap, and increase number of sc around armholes accordingly.

Using larger hook, with RS facing, join yarn with sl st in center base ch of one underarm.

Rnd 1 (RS): Ch 1, sc in same ch, sc in remaining 3 (3, 3, 3, 5, 5, 5, 7, 7, 7) base ch, sc evenly along armhole shaping by working 2 sc in each dc row edge, sc in each sc row edge, sc in sc row edge of base ch/sc. For Strap, ch 1, BASE CH/SC 26 (26, 26, 28, 28, 28, 28, 30, 30, 30) to measure approximately 8 (8, 8, 8½, 8½, 8½, 8½, 9, 9, 9)" (20.5 [20.5, 20.5, 21.5, 21.5, 21.5, 21.5, 23, 23, 23]cm) slightly stretched, join to other

edge of same armhole by working sc in sc row edge of base ch/sc, sc in next sc row edge, 2 sc in each dc row edge, sc in sc row edge at Row 5, sc in remaining 3 (3, 3, 3, 5, 5, 5, 7, 7, 7) base ch at underarm, sl st in beg sc, turn.

Change to smaller hook, working to tighter gauge to control excessive stretch in Straps.

Rnd 2 (WS): Ch 1, sc in each sc to Strap, sc in each sc of Strap, sc in each sc to end, sl st in beg sc, turn.

Rnd 3: Ch 1, sc in each sc around, sl st in beg sc, fasten off.

Make the second strap in the same way.

NECK EDGE

Using the smaller hook, finish neckline.

With RS facing, join yarn with sl st in center back neck base ch.

Rnd 1 (RS): Ch 1, sc in same ch, sc in each remaining base ch of back neck, sc in each base ch of strap, sc in each base ch of front neck, sc in each base ch of other strap, sc in each remaining base ch of back neck, sl st in beg sc, turn.

Rnd 2: Ch 1, sc in each sc, sl st in beg sc, turn.

Rnd 3: Repeat Rnd 2, fasten off.

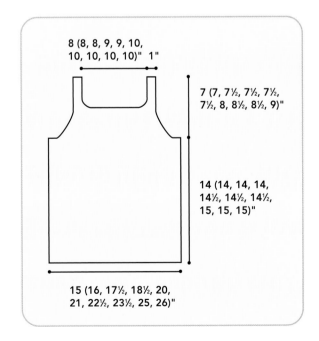

8 (8, 8, 9, 9, 10, 10, 10, 10, 10)" 1"

7 (7, 7½, 7½, 7½, 7½, 8, 8½, 8½, 9)"

14 (14, 14, 14, 14½, 14½, 14½, 15, 15, 15)"

15 (16, 17½, 18½, 20, 21, 22½, 23½, 25, 26)"

| Skill Level | INTERMEDIATE | 4 MEDIUM |

Size

Finished bust: 30 (32, 35, 37, 40, 42, 45, 47, 50, 52)" (76 [81, 88, 94, 101.5, 106.5, 114, 119, 127, 132]cm)

Materials

South West Trading Company Oasis; 100% soy silk; 3½ oz (100g)/240 yd (219m)

2 (3, 3, 3, 3, 4, 4, 4, 5, 5) balls in Chocolate

Size G-7 (4.5mm) crochet hook

Size G-6 (4mm) crochet hook for finishing

Gauge

Using larger hook, 13 BASE CH/SC = 4" (10cm)

In shell pattern, 2 repeats = 2½" (6.5cm); 6 rows = 2½" (6.5cm) unstretched

Using smaller hook, 14 sc = 4" (10cm)

Special Stitches

See Cameo, page 21

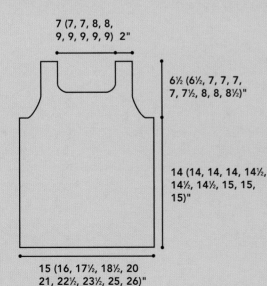

7 (7, 7, 8, 8, 9, 9, 9, 9, 9) 2"

6½ (6½, 7, 7, 7, 7, 7½, 8, 8, 8½)"

14 (14, 14, 14, 14½, 14½, 14½, 15, 15, 15)"

15 (16, 17½, 18½, 20 21, 22½, 23½, 25, 26)"

SWEET TEA

For more coverage, simply crochet more around the neck and armholes of Cameo and you get Sweet Tea. Size the tank up and get a cool vest. Or, instead of sizing up for a looser layering piece, play with gauging up: Make the same size but use slightly thicker yarn, for instance DK or light worsted weight.

INSTRUCTIONS

This version features 2" (5cm) wide straps, with 7 rounds sc at the armhole, 5 rounds sc at the neck. Work same as Cameo (page 20), sizing bust and length as desired, up to Finishing for Straps and Neck Edge.

WIDE STRAP

Rnd 1–3: Same as narrow Cameo Strap (page 23), except at end of last round, do not fasten off. Turn.

Rnd 4–7: Ch 1, sc in each sc around, sl st in beg sc, turn, fasten off.

Make second strap in same way.

NECK EDGE

Rnd 1–3: Same as Cameo Neck Edge (page 23), except do not fasten off. Turn.

Rnd 4–5: Ch 1, sc in each sc around, sl st in beg sc, turn, fasten off.

SOMNAMBULISTA

Add a shaped longer body and a peek-a-boo lace hem to the basic Cami-Tank and you have a breezy little nightgown or a pretty A-line tunic. For more ease as sleepwear, I suggest you size up and make sure it finishes to fingertip length; it'll just cover the butt. The yarn, a comfortable and breathable bamboo fiber, has a crisp, cool hand at first, but will become softer the more it's washed.

| Skill Level | INTERMEDIATE | 4 MEDIUM |

Size

Finished bust: 30 (32, 35, 37, 40, 42, 45, 47, 50, 52)" (76 [81, 88, 94, 101.5, 106.5, 114, 119, 127, 132]cm)

Materials

South West Trading Company Bamboo; 100% bamboo; 3½ oz (100 g)/250 yd (228m)

3 (3, 4, 4, 4, 5, 5, 5, 6, 6) balls in Sky

Size G-7 (4.5mm) crochet hook

Size G-6 (4mm) crochet hook for finishing

Gauge

Using larger hook, 13 BASE CH/SC = 4" (10cm)

In shell pattern, 2 repeats = 2½" (6.5cm); 6 rows = 2½" (6.5cm) unstretched

Using smaller hook, 14 sc = 4" (10cm)

Special Stitches

See Cameo, page 21

INSTRUCTIONS

Make same as Cameo (page 20) through Body Rnd 3, making bust short rows if desired. **Note:** If you made C and D short rows, ignore the sl sts and work the next round in pattern as facing.

BODY CONTINUED

There is a shell at center of underarm; 24 (26, 28, 30, 32, 34, 36, 38, 40, 42) pattern repeats. Work even until past the fullness of the bust, but stop a couple of inches before the waist. This runs from 4 to 6 or more inches (10–15cm) below the underarm.

Beginning by working PATT RND 2, work even for 7 (8, 8, 9, 8, 8, 9, 10, 10, 11) more rows. End by working PATT ROW 2 (1, 1, 2, 1, 1, 2, 1, 1, 2).

Adjusting torso length

Few figures may actually need this, but if you are especially short or long in the torso: For Petite or a short torso, omit 2 rounds (approximately 1" [2.5cm]). For Tall or a long torso, add 2 rounds (approximately 1" [2.5cm]).

A-LINE SKIRT

Begin A-line shaping, setting up four increase corners. Mark the center st of each increase corner as you make it in the following row, and move or wrap markers up as you go.

Stitch Pattern

A-LINE SHAPE

A-LINE 1 (inc) (as PATT RND 1): Ch 3, *work in pattern to next marked corner sc, INC-SH in corner sc*; repeat from * to * 3 times, work in pattern to end, ending with (dc, ch 1, dc) in same sc as beg, sc in top of beg ch, turn.

A-LINE 2 (even) (as PATT RND 2): Ch 1, sc in next dc, *work in pattern to next inc-sh, over inc-sh work [sc in second dc, SH in third dc, sc in fourth dc]*; repeat from * to * 3 times, work in pattern to end, ending with sl st in beg sc, turn.

A-LINE 3 (inc) (as PATT RND 2): Ch 1, sc in next dc, *work in pattern to next marked corner sc, INC-SH in corner sc*; repeat from * to * 3 times, work in pattern to end, ending with sl st in beg sc, turn.

A-LINE 4 (even) (as PATT RND 1): Ch 3, *work in pattern to next inc-sh, over inc-sh work [sc in second dc, SH in third dc, sc in 4th dc]*; repeat from * to * 3 times, work in pattern to end, ending with (dc, ch 1, dc) in same sc as beg, sc in top of beg ch, turn.

Sizes 30 (37, 45, 52)

Foundation Rnd (inc): Ch 3, *[sc in second dc of next shell, SH in next sc] 3 (4, 5, 6) times, sc in second dc of next shell, INC-SH in next sc for corner*; repeat from * to *, repeat between [ ] 4 (5, 6, 7) times, repeat from * to * twice, repeat between [ ] 3 (4, 5, 6) times, sc in second dc of next shell, (dc, ch 1, dc) in same sc as beg, sc in top of beg ch, turn.

Work A-LINE 2, PATT RNDS 1–2 for 3 times, PATT RND 1 once more, A-LINE RNDS 3–4, PATT RND 2, PATT RNDS 1–2 for 3 times, A-LINE 1–2, PATT RNDS 1–2 for 4 (4, 4, 5) times.

Sizes 32 (35, 40, 42, 47, 50)

Foundation Rnd (inc): Ch 1, sc in next dc, *[SH in next sc, sc in second dc of next shell] 4 (4, 5, 5, 6, 6) times, INC-SH in next sc, sc in second dc of next shell, repeat between [ ] 3 (4, 4, 5, 5, 6) times, INC-SH in next sc, sc in second dc of next shell, repeat between [ ] 4 (4, 5, 5, 6, 6) times*; repeat from * to *, except omit last sc, instead end with sl st in beg sc, turn.

Work A-LINE 4, PATT RND 2, PATT RNDS 1–2 for 3 times, A-LINE 1–2, PATT RNDS 1–2 for 3 times, PATT RND 1 once more, A-LINE 3–4, PATT RND 2, PATT RNDS 1–2 for 3 (3, 3, 3, 4, 4) times.

36 (38, 40, 42, 44, 46, 48, 50, 52, 54) pattern repeats.

Adjusting skirt length

For Petite or shorter tunic: Omit 2 rounds (approximately 1" [2.5cm]) or more, end by working PATT RND 2. For Tall or longer tunic: Add 2 rounds (approximately 1" [2.5cm]) or more, end by working PATT RND 2. For the same length tunic without lace trim, repeat the last 2 rounds 4 times (approximately 3" [7.5cm]) or to desired length.

TRIM

Scallop lace trim is crocheted in joined rounds, RS always facing. Turn, RS now facing, regardless of previous designation. There is a sc at center of underarm. Set up 18 (19, 20, 21, 22, 23, 24, 25, 26, 27) scallop repeats.

Rnd 1: Ch 3, dc in same sc, *ch 3, sk (dc, ch 1, dc) of next shell, sc in next ch-1 sp, sc in next dc, sc in next sc, sc in first dc of next shell, sc in next ch-1 sp, ch 3, sk remaining (dc, ch 1, dc) of shell, TSH in next sc*; repeat from * to * to end, except omit last TSH, instead end with 2 dc in same sc as beg, ch 1, sc in top of beg ch—18 (19, 20, 21, 22, 23, 24, 25, 26, 27) pattern repeats.

Rnd 2: Ch 3, (dc, ch 2, 2 dc) in first sp, *ch 3, sk next sc, sc in each of next 3 sc, ch 3, sk next sc, [TSH, ch 2, TSH] in next ch-2 sp of shell*; repeat from * to * to end, except omit last repeat of [ ], instead end with TSH in same sp as beg, ch 1, sc in top of beg ch.

Rnd 3: Ch 3, dc in first sp, ch 2, *TSH in next ch-2 sp of shell, ch 3, sk next sc, sc in next sc, ch 3, sk next sc, TSH in next ch-2 sp of shell, ch 2, TSH in next ch-2 sp between shells, ch 2*; repeat from * to * to end, except omit last shell, instead end with 2 dc in same sp as beg, ch 1, sc in top of beg ch.

Rnd 4: Ch 3, (dc, ch 2, 2 dc) in first sp, ch 3, *TSH in next ch-2 sp of shell, ch 3, sc in next sc, ch 3, [TSH in next ch-2 sp of shell, ch 3] twice*; repeat from * to * to end, sl st in top of beg ch, fasten off.

FINISHING
STRAPS AND NECK EDGE

Note: RS of Trim will determine RS for finishing. Make narrow Straps and Neck Edge same as Cameo (page 23), adjusting for fit.

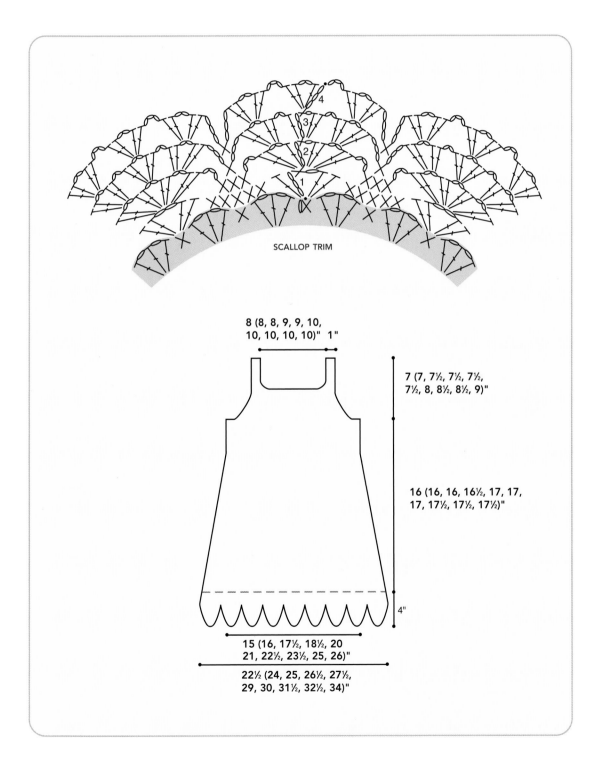

SCALLOP TRIM

8 (8, 8, 9, 9, 10, 10, 10, 10, 10)" 1"

7 (7, 7½, 7½, 7½, 7½, 8, 8½, 8½, 9)"

16 (16, 16, 16½, 17, 17, 17, 17½, 17½, 17½)"

4"

15 (16, 17½, 18½, 20 21, 22½, 23½, 25, 26)"

22½ (24, 25, 26½, 27½, 29, 30, 31½, 32½, 34)"

|3|
TOPS OF THE LINE
PULLOVERS

Unless you are built like a Vargas babe, clingy sweaters are not attractive. Crocheted sweaters often turn out just the opposite: thick and clunky, also not attractive. But choosing the right yarn, working a breathable, stretchy stitch pattern, and making your personal fitting adjustments can result in a truly flattering sweater that will win you raves.

What follows is a romp through several variations on the pullover theme. With specific sample garments, I'll illustrate a few different ways to finish your pullover. But ultimately, you will have all the tools you need to put together the parts that work best for your figure.

YARN NOTES

You may use a wide range of yarn thicknesses, from light to DK to worsted weight, ball band symbol 3 to 4, with a knitting gauge of 5 to 5½ sts per inch (2.5cm). Crocheting to the stated gauge with a finer or silkier yarn produces a lighter, lacier top (see Runaround, page 46, or Rah-boon-dee-ay, page 58). Choose a yarn on the bulkier side and crochet to the same gauge for a dense sweater (see No Sweat, page 42).

If you can't hit the gauge using your yarn, but it's just the tiniest bit too small (no smaller than 2¾" [7cm] per 2 repeats/6 rows), you can still work this pattern. It will be a bit tighter. If that's not what you want, then size up.

If you can't hit the gauge using your yarn, but it's just the tiniest bit too big (but no bigger than 3¼" [8cm] per 2 repeats/6 rows) you can still work this pattern, too. You will gain some extra ease for the size you make: as much as 4" (10cm) in the largest sizes. That means you do not have to size up for a roomy sweater. Make the size closest to your bust measurement, and let your gauge create the added ease.

In either case, you should be prepared to adjust the length if needed.

SIZE FINDER

For a next-to-the body top, choose the size closest to your bust measurement. Size up or gauge up for a sweater layer. For a longer sweater where hips are an issue, add the hip shaping as in Tall Latte (page 50) or the side vents as in No Sweat (page 42).

JEWEL

As I have matured, I have found I don't enjoy
wearing anything that binds. Jewel is my most
comfortable top, featuring a nicely open neckline
and the three-quarter sleeve that many crocheters
have requested, the solution for those of us who
are constantly pushing up our sleeves to wash our
hands, do dishes, or eat pasta.

JEWEL

Skill Level	INTERMEDIATE	3 LIGHT

Size
Finished bust: 33 (36, 39, 42, 45, 48, 51, 54)" (84 [91, 99, 106.5, 114, 122, 129.5, 137]cm)

Materials
Classic Elite Premier; 50% Pima cotton, 50% Tencel; 1¾ oz (50g)/108 yd (99m)

7 (8, 9, 11, 12, 13, 14, 15) hanks in #5295 Eggplant

Size I-9 (5.5mm) crochet hook

Size H-9 (5mm) crochet hook for finishing

Gauge
11 BASE CH/SC = 4" (10cm)

In shell pattern, 2 repeats (SH, sc) and 6 rows = 3" (7.5cm)

In sc, worked firmly for finishing, using smaller hook if needed, 12 sc = 4" (10cm)

INSTRUCTIONS

Here's the construction for a comfortable, generous neckline that is more open than a traditional jewel neck but not quite as wide as a boat neck. It is also used for No Sweat (page 42) and Runaround (page 46).

YOKE
BASE CH/SC 41 (41, 41, 41, 41, 45, 45, 45) to measure approximately 15 (15, 15, 15, 15, 16, 16, 16)" (38 [38, 38, 38, 38, 40.5, 40.5, 40.5]cm) slightly stretched.
Although not technically rounds, call the next three RNDS 1–3.

Sizes 33 (36, 39)
Rnd 1: Ch 3, (dc, ch 1, 2 dc) in first sc, [sk next sc, sc in next sc, sk next sc, SH in next sc] 10 times, placing SH in last sc, turn—11 shells.
Rnd 2 (inc): Ch 3, (dc, ch 1, 2 dc) in first dc, sc in next ch-sp of sh, *INC-SH in next sc for corner, sc in next ch-sp of sh*, [SH in next sc, sc in next ch-sp of sh], repeat from * to *, repeat between [ ] 4 times, repeat from * to *, repeat between [ ], repeat from * to *, end with SH in top of tch, turn—12 shells.
Complete neckline and join front neck with additional sts.
Rnd 3 (inc): Ch 3, (dc, ch 1, 2 dc) in first dc, *[sc in next ch-sp of sh, SH in next sc] to next inc-sh, over inc-sh work (sc in first ch-sp, INC-SH in next ch-sp, sc in next ch-sp), SH in next sc*; repeat from * to * 3 times, sc in ch-sp of last sh, SH in top of tch, ch 1, BASE CH/SC 9 for front neck, sl st in top of beg ch, fasten off.

Special Stitches

SH: (2 dc, ch 1, 2 dc) in same st or sp

INC-SH: [Dc, (ch 1, dc) 3 times] in same st or sp

Stitch Pattern Notes

This is a pattern of staggered shells separated by sc.

STITCH PATTERN (IN ROWS)

PATT ROW 1: Ch 1, sc in first dc, [SH in next sc, sc in next ch-sp of sh] across, placing last sc in top of tch, turn.

PATT ROW 2: Ch 3, 2 dc in first sc, [sc in next ch-sp of sh, SH in next sc] across, except omit last SH, instead end with 3 dc in last sc, turn.

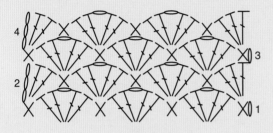

SHELL PATTERN IN ROWS

STITCH PATTERN (IN ROUNDS)

PATT RND 1: Ch 1, sc in same ch-sp, [SH in next sc, sc in next ch-sp of sh] around, except omit last sc, instead end with sl st in beg sc, turn.

PATT RND 2: Ch 3, dc in same sc, [sc in next ch-sp of sh, SH in next sc] around, except omit last SH, instead end with 2 dc in same sc as beg, sc in top of beg ch, turn.

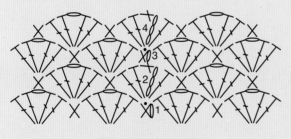

SHELL PATTERN IN RNDS

YOKE INCREASE PATTERN (IN ROUNDS)

Note: These increase patterns are used on the Jewel Neck Yoke only. YOKE RNDS 1–3 are worked successively to inc 1 shell over 3 rounds.

YOKE RND 1 (inc): Starting in corner sc, ch 4 (counts as dc, ch 1), dc in same sc (half of inc-sh made), *sc in next ch-sp of sh, [SH in next sc, sc in next ch-sp of sh] to next corner sc, INC-SH in corner sc*; repeat from * to * 3 times, except omit last INC-SH, instead end with (dc, ch 1, dc) in same sc as beg, sc in third ch of beg ch (corner inc-sh complete), turn.

YOKE RND 2 (even): Ch 3, dc in same ch-sp, sc in next ch-sp, *SH in next sc, [sc in next ch-sp of sh, SH in next sc] to next inc-sh**, over inc-sh work (sc in first ch-sp, SH in next ch-sp, sc in next ch-sp)*; repeat from * to * twice, repeat from * ending at **, sc in next ch-sp, end with 2 dc in same ch-sp as beg, sc in top of beg ch, turn.

YOKE RND 3 (even): PATT RND 1.

Note: YOKE RND 4 is worked over an increase round to produce an extra increase of 1 shell in 1 round.

YOKE RND 4 (inc rnd over inc rnd): Starting in corner sc, ch 4 (counts as dc, ch 1), dc in same sc (half of inc-sh made), *SH in next sc, [sc in next ch-sp of sh, SH in next sc] to next inc-sh**, over inc-sh work (sc in first ch-sp, INC-SH in next ch-sp, sc in next ch-sp)*; repeat from * to * twice, repeat from * ending at **, sc in next ch-sp, end with [dc, ch 1, dc] in same ch-sp as beg, sc in third ch of beg ch, turn.

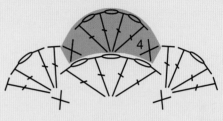

YOKE INCREASE PATTERN

TAPER PATTERN (FOR SLEEVES, IN ROUNDS, DECREASES ONE PATTERN REPEAT)

TAPER 1: Ch 3, [sc in next ch-sp of sh, SH in next sc] around, except omit last SH, instead end with dc in same sc as beg, sc in top of beg ch, turn.

TAPER 2: Ch 1, sc in same ch-sp, (dc, ch 1, dc) in next sc, [sc in next ch-sp of sh, SH in next sc] around, except omit last SH, instead (dc, ch 1, dc) in last sc, sl st in beg sc, turn.

TAPER 3: Ch 1, sc in same sc, sk (dc, ch 1, dc), [SH in next sc, sc in next ch-sp of sh] around, SH in last sc, sk (dc, ch 1, dc), sl st in beg sc, turn.

TAPER 4: PATT RND 2.

TAPER 5: PATT RND 1.

TAPER PATTERN

Sizes 42 (45)

For the first row only, make an additional increase at center back neck.

Rnd 1: Ch 3, (dc, ch 1, 2 dc) in first sc, [sk next sc, sc in next sc, sk next sc, SH in next sc] 4 times, sk next sc, sc in next sc, sk next sc, INC-SH in next sc, repeat between [ ] 5 times, placing SH in last sc, turn—11 shells.

Rnd 2 (inc): Ch 3, (dc, ch 1, 2 dc) in first dc, *sc in next ch-sp of sh, INC-SH in next sc for corner; [sc in next ch-sp of sh, SH in next sc]*, repeat from * to *, repeat between [ ] to inc-sh at center back, over inc-sh work (sc in first ch-sp, SH in next ch-sp, sc in next ch-sp), SH in next sc. Repeat between [ ], repeat from * to * twice, placing last SH in top of tch, turn—13 pattern repeats.

Rnd 3 (inc): Same as Size 33 Rnd 3, except BASE CH/SC 11 for front neck.

Size 48

Rnd 1: Ch 3, (dc, ch 1, 2 dc) in first sc, [sk next sc, sc in next sc, sk next sc, SH in next sc] 11 times, placing SH in last sc, turn—12 pattern repeats.

Rnd 2 (inc): Ch 3, (dc, ch 1, 2 dc) in first dc, sc in next ch-sp of sh, *INC-SH in next sc for corner, sc in next ch-sp of sh*, [SH in next sc, sc in next ch-sp of sh], repeat from * to *, repeat between [ ] 5 times, repeat from * to *, repeat between [ ], repeat from * to *, end with SH in top of tch, turn—13 pattern repeats.

Rnd 3 (inc): Same as Size 33 Rnd 3, except BASE CH/SC 11 for front neck.

Sizes 51 (54)

Rnd 1: Same as Size 48 Rnd 1—12 pattern repeats. For the next row only, make an additional increase at the center back neck.

Rnd 2 (inc): Ch 3, (dc, ch 1, 2 dc) in first dc, sc in next ch-sp of sh, *INC-SH in next sc for corner, sc in next ch-sp of sh*, [SH in next sc, sc in next ch-sp of sh], repeat from * to *, repeat between [ ] 2 times, repeat from * to *, repeat between [ ] 2 times, repeat from * to *, repeat between [ ], repeat from * to *, repeat be-

tween [ ], end with SH in top of tch, turn—13 shells.

Rnd 3 (inc): Ch 3, (dc, ch 1, 2 dc) in first dc, *[sc in next ch-sp of sh, SH in next sc] to next inc-sh, over inc-sh work (sc in first ch-sp, INC-SH in next ch-sp, sc in next ch-sp), SH in next sc*; repeat from * to *, repeat between [ ] to inc-sh at center back, work (sc in first ch-sp, SH in next ch-sp, sc in next ch-sp), SH in next sc, repeat from * to * twice, sc in ch-sp of last sh, SH in top of tch, ch 1, BASE CH/SC 15 for front neck, sl st in top of beg ch, fasten off.

All Sizes

Turn, sk next corner of front, join with sl st in corner ch-sp of next inc-sh at back, now working across back.

Size 33

Rnd 4 (even): Ch 3, dc in same ch-sp, sc in next ch-sp of inc-sh, SH in next sc, *[sc in next ch-sp of sh, SH in next sc] to next inc-sh, over inc-sh work (sc in first ch-sp, SH in next ch-sp, sc in next ch-sp), SH in next sc*; repeat from * to *, repeat between [ ] to sh before front neck, sc in ch-sp of sh, sk next sc of front neck, SH next sc, sk next 2 sc, sc in next sc, sk next 2 sc, SH in next sc, sk remaining sc, repeat from * to *, repeat between [ ] to beg inc-sh, sc in last ch-sp, end with 2 dc in same sp as beg, sc in top of beg ch, turn.

Rnd 5–13: YOKE RND 3, YOKE RNDS 1–3 twice, YOKE RNDS 1–2 once more—34 pattern repeats.

Size 36

Rnd 4 (inc): Ch 4 (counts as dc, ch 1), dc in same ch-sp, sc in next ch-sp of inc-sh, SH in next sc, *[sc in next ch-sp of sh, SH in next sc] to next inc-sh, over inc-sh work (sc in first ch-sp, INC-SH in next ch-sp, sc in next ch-sp), SH in next sc*; repeat from * to *, repeat between [ ] to sh before front neck, sc in ch-sp of sh, sk next sc of front neck, SH next sc, sk next 2 sc, sc in next sc, sk next 2 sc, SH in next sc, sk remaining sc, repeat from * to *, repeat between [ ] to beg, sc in last ch-sp, end with (dc, ch 1, dc) in same sp as beg, sc in top of beg ch, turn.

Rnd 5–14: YOKE RNDS 2–3, YOKE RNDS 1–2 twice, YOKE RNDS 1–2 once more—38 pattern repeats.

Size 39

Rnd 4: Same as Size 36 Rnd 4.

Rnd 5–15: YOKE RND 4, YOKE RNDS 2–3, YOKE RNDS 1–3 twice, YOKE RNDS 1–2 once more—42 pattern repeats.

Size 42 (45)

Rnd 4: Same as Size 36 Rnd 4, except over 11 sc of front neck work [sk first sc of front neck, (SH in next sc, sk next sc, sc in next sc, sk next sc) twice, SH in next sc, sk remaining sc].

Rnd 5–15: Same as Size 39 Rnds 5–15—44 pattern repeats.

Size 48

Rnd 4: Same as Size 42 Rnd 4.

Rnd 5–16: YOKE RND 4 for twice, YOKE RNDS 2–3, YOKE RNDS 1–3 twice, YOKE RNDS 1–2 once more—48 pattern repeats.

Size 51

Rnd 4: Same as Size 36 Rnd 4, except over 15 sc of front neck work [sk first sc for front neck, (SH in next sc, sk next sc, sc in next sc, sk next sc) 3 times, SH in next sc, sk remaining sc].

Rnd 5–16: Same as Size 48 Rnds 5–16—50 pattern repeats.

Size 54

Rnd 4: Same as Size 51 Rnd 4.

Rnd 5–17: YOKE RND 4 for 3 times, YOKE RNDS 2–3, YOKE RNDS 1–3 twice, YOKE RNDS 1–2 once more—54 pattern repeats.

JOINING

There is a shell at each corner. Join front and back with additional stitches at underarms. SIZES 33 (39, 42, 45, 54) begin by working across back; SIZES 36 (48, 51) begin by making underarm ch.

Sizes 33 (39, 42, 45, 54)

Join Rnd: Ch 1, sc in same ch-sp, *work in pattern to next corner sh, sc in ch-sp of corner sh, ch 1, BASE CH/SC 7 (7, 7, 11, 11) for underarm, sk next 6 (8, 8, 8, 10) sh of armhole, sc in ch-sp of next corner sh*; repeat from * to *, except omit last sc, instead end with sl st in beg sc, fasten off.

Sizes 36 (48, 51)

Join Rnd: Ch 1, sc in same ch-sp, *ch 1, BASE CH/SC 7 (11, 11) for underarm, sk next 7 (9, 9) sh of armhole, sc in ch-sp of next corner sh, work in pattern to next corner sh, sc in ch-sp of corner sh*; repeat from * to *, except omit last sc, instead end with sl st in beg sc, fasten off.

BODY

Move join to center of underarm, now working toward front. SIZES 33 (39, 42, 45, 54) turn, go to center of same underarm; SIZES 36 (48, 51) turn, sk across the back, go to center of next underarm.

Sizes 33 (36, 39, 42)

Rnd 1: Join with sl st in 4th sc at center of underarm, ch 1, sc in same sc, *sk remaining 3 sc of underarm, SH in next sc, work in pattern, placing SH in sc before next underarm, sk next 3 sc, sc in next sc*; repeat from * to *, except omit last sc, instead end with sl st in beg sc, turn.

Sizes 45 (48, 51, 54)

Rnd 1: Join with sl st in 6th sc at center of underarm, ch 3, dc in same sc, *sk next 2 sc, sc in next sc, sk remaining 2 sc, SH in next sc, work in pattern, placing SH in sc before next underarm, sk next 2 sc, sc in next sc, sk next 2 sc, SH in next sc*; repeat from * to * except omit last SH, instead end with 2 dc in same sc as beg, sc in top of beg ch, turn.

Work one round even on 22 (24, 26, 28, 30, 32, 34, 36) pattern repeats, working now toward back, as follows.

Sizes 33 (36, 39, 42)

Rnd 2: PATT RND 2.

Sizes 45 (48, 51, 54)

Rnd 2: PATT RND 1.

Adjusting for full bust

Turn, now moving toward the front. All sizes are at the center stitch at underarm; for SIZES 33 (36, 39, 42) that is a shell, for SIZES 45 (48, 51, 54) that is a sc. Put the loop on the hook on hold.

SIZES 33 (36, 39, 42) sk same sh, join new yarn with sl st in ch-sp of next shell. SIZES 45 (48, 51, 54) sk next sh, join with sl st in ch-sp of next shell.

Short Row A: [SH in next sc, sc in ch-sp of next shell] 9 (10, 11, 12, 12, 13, 14, 15) times across front, except omit last sc, instead end with sl st in ch-sp of sh, turn.

Short Row B: Sl st in each of next 2 dc, sl st in next ch-sp of sh, [SH in next sc, sc in next ch-sp of sh] 8 (9, 10, 11, 11, 12, 13, 14) times, except omit last sc, instead end with sl st in ch-sp sh, fasten off. Put the loop on hold back on the hook.

Note: If you made A and B short rows, ignore the sl sts and work the next round in pattern as facing.

Stop here for No Sweat, continued on page 44, and Runaround, page 48. **Stop here for No Sweat, continued on page 44, and Runaround, page 48.**

BODY CONTINUED

The remainder of the body is straight, unshaped to hip length.

Rnd 3–28: Begin with PATT RND 1 (1, 1, 1, 2, 2, 2, 2), alternating PATT RNDS 1–2, work even on 22 (24, 26, 28, 30, 32, 34, 36) pattern repeats for 26 more rounds, or to desired length. Fasten off.

SLEEVES

Facing opposite direction of armhole stitches, join with sl st in 4th (4th, 4th, 4th, 6th, 6th, 6th, 6th) base ch at center of underarm.

Sizes 33 (36, 39, 42)

Rnd 1: Ch 3, dc in same ch, sk remaining 3 ch of underarm, sc in marked corner ch-sp, work in pattern across armhole, placing sc in next marked corner ch-sp, sk next 3 ch of underarm, 2 dc in same ch as beg, ch 1, sc in top of beg ch, turn—8 (9, 10, 10) pattern repeats.

Sizes 45 (48, 51, 54)

Rnd 1: Ch 1, sc in same ch, sk next 2 ch, SH in next ch, sk remaining 2 ch, sc in marked corner ch-sp, work in pattern across armhole, placing sc in next marked corner ch-sp, sk next 2 ch of underarm, SH in next ch, sk rem 2 ch, sl st in beg sc, turn—11 (12, 12, 13) pattern repeats.

All Sizes

The Jewel sleeve is full-width, three-quarter length.

Rnd 2–22: Begin with PATT RND 1 (1, 1, 1, 2, 2, 2, 2). Alternating PATT RNDS 1–2, work even on 8 (9, 10, 10, 11, 12, 12, 13) pattern repeats for 21 rounds, or to desired length. Fasten off.

Adjusting sleeves for width

If you are particularly ample in the upper arm, you may prefer to maintain full width through the length of the sleeve. But for less bulk in the larger sizes (optional for smaller sizes), I suggest tapering the upper arm as follows:

Sizes 48 (51)

Rnd 2–22: PATT RND 2, PATT RND 1, TAPER RNDS 1–5, PATT RND 2, repeat PATT RNDS 1–2 for 6 times,

PATT RND 1 once more, or continue in pattern to desired length on 11 (11) pattern repeats, fasten off.

Size 54

Rnd 2–22: PATT RND 2, PATT RND 1, TAPER RNDS 1–5 twice, PATT RND 2, PATT RNDS 1–2 for 4 times, or continue in pattern to desired length on 11 pattern repeats, fasten off.

Make second sleeve in the same way.

FINISHING
NECK EDGE

Finish neck edge with a RS round of sc, working firmly to gauge of 12 sc = 4" (10cm), switching to smaller hook if needed to achieve gauge.

Neck Rnd 1: RS facing, join with sl st in 21st (21st, 21st, 21st, 21st, 23rd, 23rd, 23rd) base ch at center back of neck, ch 1, sc in same ch, sc in each remaining ch, 2 sc in each dc row edge of neck shaping, sc in each base ch of front neck, 2 sc in each dc row edge of other side neck shaping, sc in remaining base ch of back neck, sl st in beg sc—62 (62, 62, 64, 64, 68, 72, 72) sc.

Fasten off for a spare, simple edge. Or continue as instructed for the trim options in the versions that follow.

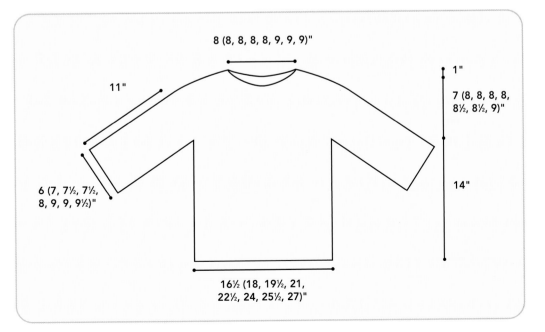

8 (8, 8, 8, 8, 9, 9, 9)"

11"

1"

7 (8, 8, 8, 8, 8½, 8½, 9)"

6 (7, 7½, 7½, 8, 9, 9, 9½)"

14"

16½ (18, 19½, 21, 22½, 24, 25½, 27)"

NO SWEAT

Turn Jewel (page 34) into the prettiest sweatshirt
you'll ever own. There's ribbing at the neck and cuffs
to keep things neat. The bottom, which hits at the
hip, is left open with side vents for ease. For a
roomier layer over other clothes, I suggest you size
up. Choosing a soft, cushy yarn that's on the bulkier
side of the range and working to the same gauge results in a denser fabric, perfect for sweats.

Skill Level | INTERMEDIATE

Size

Finished bust 33 (36, 39, 42, 45, 48, 51, 54)" (84 [91, 99, 106.5, 114, 122, 129.5, 137]cm)

Materials

Classic Elite Patina; 70% cotton, 30% silk, 1¾ oz (50g)/108 yd (99m)

10 (11, 12, 13, 14, 15, 16, 18) balls in #7373 Tourmaline

Size I-9 (5.5mm) crochet hook

Size H-9 (5mm) crochet hook for finishing

Gauge

11 BASE CH/SC = 4" (10cm)

In shell pattern, 2 repeats (SH, sc) and 6 rows = 3" (7.5cm)

In sc, worked firmly for finishing, using smaller hook if needed, 12 sc = 4" (10cm)

In FP/BP ribbing, using smaller hook, 12 st = 4" (10cm), 10 rows = 3" (7.5cm)

Special Stitches

See Jewel, page 37

FPdc (front post double crochet): YO, insert hook from front to back to front again around the post of next st, YO, draw yarn through st, (YO, draw yarn through 2 loops on hook) twice.

BPdc (back post double crochet): YO, insert hook from back to front to back again around the post of next st, YO, draw yarn through st, (YO, draw yarn through 2 loops on hook) twice.

INSTRUCTIONS

YOKE

Same as Jewel (page 36) through Joining and Body Rnd 2, making bust short rows if desired.

BODY

Work even on 22 (24, 26, 28, 30, 32, 34, 36) pattern repeats until approximately 11" (28cm) from underarms, 21 or 22 more rounds, or to desired length before Side Vents. End by working PATT RND 1.

SIDE VENTS

Divide front and back and work each half separately for approximately 4" (10cm), or for desired length.

FIRST SIDE

Row 1: Ch 3, 2 dc in same sc, [sc in next ch-sp of sh, SH in next sc] 10 (11, 12, 13, 14, 15, 16, 17) times, except omit last SH, instead 3 dc in next sc, turn—10 (11, 12, 13, 14, 15, 16, 17) pattern repeats. (Note: If hip shaping has been done prior to Side Vents, work 2 extra shells in Row 1 to end at center sc on side.)

Row 2–8: PATT ROW 1–2 for 3 times, PATT ROW 1 once more, fasten off.

SECOND SIDE

Join with sl st in same sc as last 3 dc of First Side Row 1. Make same way as first side.

SLEEVES

No Sweat has long sleeves and ribbed cuffs. All sizes except Size 33 have gradually tapered sleeves.

Rnd 1: Make sleeve on armhole same as Jewel Rnd 1 (page 40)—8 (9, 10, 10, 11, 12, 12, 13) pattern repeats.

Size 33

PATT RNDS 1–2 for 14 times.

Size 36

PATT RNDS 1–2 for 6 times, PATT RND 1, TAPER 1–5, PATT RND 2, PATT RND 1–2 for 4 times.

Sizes 39 (42)

PATT RNDS 1–2 for 4 times, PATT RND 1, TAPER 1–5 twice, PATT RND 2, PATT RNDS 1–2 for 4 times.

Sizes 45 (48, 51)

PATT RND 2, PATT RNDS 1–2 twice, PATT RND 1, TAPER 1–5 for 3 times, PATT RND 2, PATT RNDS 1–2 for 3 times.

Size 54

PATT RND 2, PATT RND 1, TAPER 1–5 for 4 times, PATT RND 2, PATT RNDS 1–2 twice.

8 (8, 8, 8, 8, 9, 9, 9) pattern repeats.

Adjusting for length

Shorten or lengthen sleeve before cuff by omitting or adding rounds. End by working PATT RND 2.

CUFF

All sizes turn, RS now facing, gently gather the sleeve bottom with 3 sc over each pattern repeat, working firmly to gauge of 12 sc = 4" (10cm), switching to smaller hook if needed.

Rnd 1 (RS): Ch 1, sc in same ch-sp, [sk next dc, sc in next dc, sk next sc, sc in next dc, sk next dc, sc in next ch-sp] around, except omit last sc, instead sl st in beg sc, do not turn—24 (24, 24, 24, 24, 27, 27, 27) sc.

Sizes 33 (36, 39, 42, 45)

Rnd 2 (RS): Ch 2 (counts as st), FPdc post of same sc, [BPdc next sc, FPdc next sc] 11 times, sk last sc post under beg ch, sl st in top of beg ch—24 sts.

Sizes 48 (51, 54)

Rnd 2 (RS): Ch 2 (counts as st), FPdc post of same sc, [BPdc next sc, FPdc next sc] 13 times, placing last FPdc in last sc post under beg ch, sl st in top of beg ch—28 sts.

Rnd 3–10 (RS): Ch 2, [FPdc next FPdc, BPdc next BPdc] around, except FPdc last FPdc, sl st in top of beg ch, fasten off.

Make second sleeve and cuff in the same way.

COLLAR

The collar is a 1" (2.5cm) band of ribbing. Switch to smaller hook and work firmly to gauge of 12 sts = 4" (10cm).

Rnd 1 (RS): Same as Jewel Neck Edge Rnd 1 (page 41). Do not fasten off, do not turn.

Rnd 2 (RS): Ch 2 (counts as st), FPdc post of same sc, [BPdc next sc, FPdc next sc] around, sk last sc post under beg ch, sl st in top of beg ch—62 (62, 62, 64, 64, 68, 72, 72) sts.

Rnd 3–4 (RS): Ch 2, [FPdc next FPdc, BPdc next BPdc] around, ending with FPdc last FPdc, sl st in top of beg ch, fasten off.

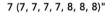

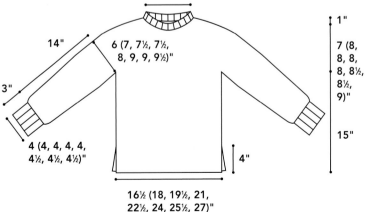

7 (7, 7, 7, 7, 8, 8, 8)"

14"

6 (7, 7½, 7½, 8, 9, 9, 9½)"

3"

1"

7 (8, 8, 8, 8½, 8½, 9)"

15"

4 (4, 4, 4, 4, 4½, 4½, 4½)"

4"

16½ (18, 19½, 21, 22½, 24, 25½, 27)"

RUNAROUND

This top is Jewel (page 34) morphed into a crew neck with mini-sleeves and a cluster-band trim. See how choosing yarn that's on the lighter side and working to the same gauge results in a lighter top. This yarn, a blend of cotton and acrylic, has the added bonus of being machine washable, which is most appreciated for a top as useful as this one.

RUNAROUND

Skill Level	INTERMEDIATE	4 MEDIUM

Size

Finished bust: 33 (36, 39, 42, 45, 48, 51, 54)" (84 [91, 99, 106.5, 114, 122, 129.5, 137]cm)

Materials

Plymouth Wildflower DK; 51% cotton, 49% acrylic; 1¾ oz (50g)/136 yd (124m)

5 (6, 7, 7, 8, 9, 9, 10) skeins in #40 (natural)

Size I-9 (5.5mm) crochet hook

Size H-9 (5mm) crochet hook for finishing

Gauge

11 BASE CH/SC = 4" (10cm)

In shell pattern, 2 repeats (SH, sc) and 6 rows = 3" (7.5cm)

In sc, worked firmly for finishing, using smaller hook if needed, 12 sc = 4" (10cm)

In cluster band, using smaller hook, 12 sts or 6 repeats (CL, ch 1) = 4" (10cm)

Special Stitches

See Jewel, page 37

CL: dc3tog in same st or sp

INSTRUCTIONS

YOKE

Same as Jewel (page 36) through Joining and Body Rnd 2, making bust short rows if desired.

BODY

Work even until approximately 13" (33cm) from underarm, 24 more rounds, or to desired length.

SLEEVES

Rnd 1: Same as Jewel Rnd 1 (page 40).

Sizes 33 (36, 39, 42)
Rnd 2–3: PATT RND 1–2.

Sizes 45 (48, 51, 54)
Rnd 2–4: PATT RND 2, then PATT RND 1–2—8 (9, 10, 10, 11, 12, 12, 13) pattern repeats.

Adjusting sleeve length
Not everyone can wear a tiny cap sleeve. For a standard short sleeve work an additional 4 rounds, to approximately 4" (10cm) from underarm, ending by working PATT RND 2.

Adjusting sleeve width
If you make a 4" (10cm) sleeve, I also suggest tapering the upper arm for the largest sizes once.

Sizes 48 (51, 54)

Rnd 2–8: PATT RND 2, PATT RND 1, TAPER RNDS 1–5, PATT RND 2—11 (11, 12) pattern repeats. Adjust sts in band accordingly.

SLEEVE CLUSTER BAND

Work firmly to gauge of 12 sts = 4" (10cm), switching to smaller hook if needed. Turn, RS now facing.

Rnd 1: Ch 1, sc in same ch-sp, sc in each of next 2 dc, *[make 4 sc over next pattern repeat by working (sk next sc, sc in each of next 2 dc, sk next ch-sp, sc in each of next 2 dc)], make 5 sc over next pattern repeat by working (sk next sc, sc in each of next 2 dc, ch-sp and 2 dc)*; repeat from * to * 2 (2, 2, 2, 2, 4, 4, 4) times, repeat between [ ] 1 (2, 3, 3, 4, 1, 1, 2) times, sc in each of last 2 dc, sl st in beg sc—36 (40, 44, 44, 48, 54, 54, 58) sc.

Rnd 2: Ch 2, dc2tog in same sc (counts as first CL), [ch 1, sk next sc, CL in next sc] around, sk last sc, sc in top of beg ch—18 (20, 22, 22, 24, 27, 27, 29) clusters.

Rnd 3: Ch 1, sc in first sp, 2 sc in each ch-1 sp around, end with sc in same sp as beg, sl st in beg sc, fasten off—36 (40, 44, 44, 48, 54, 54, 58) sc.

Make second sleeve and band in the same way.

FINISHING

NECK CLUSTER BAND

Switch to smaller hook and work firmly to gauge of 12 sts = 4" (10cm).

Rnd 1 (RS): Same as Jewel Neck Edge RND 1 (page 41). Do not fasten off, do not turn—62 (62, 62, 64, 64, 68, 72, 72) sc.

Rnd 2: Same as Sleeve Cluster Band RND 2—31 (31, 31, 32, 32, 34, 36, 36) clusters.

Rnd 3: Same as Sleeve Cluster Band RND 3—62 (62, 62, 64, 64, 68, 72, 72) sc.

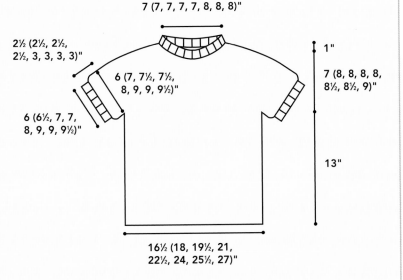

7 (7, 7, 7, 7, 8, 8, 8)"

2½ (2½, 2½, 2½, 3, 3, 3, 3)"

6 (7, 7½, 7½, 8, 9, 9, 9½)"

6 (6½, 7, 7, 8, 9, 9, 9½)"

1"

7 (8, 8, 8, 8, 8½, 8½, 9)"

13"

16½ (18, 19½, 21, 22½, 24, 25½, 27)"

TALL LATTE

A V-neck is flattering on everybody. Easygoing and sporty, this sweater features a V-neck that is quite open and low, to about the depth of the underarm. You may close the neck a bit with an optional ribbed band. The sleeves are elbow-length and also teamed with contrast banding. The sample is made at mid-hip length, with interior hip shaping for ease, but you should end your sweater at the best placement, either above or below the widest part of your lower body.

TALL LATTE

Skill Level | INTERMEDIATE | **4** MEDIUM

Size
Finished bust: 33 (36, 39, 41, 45, 48, 51, 54)" (84 [91, 99, 106.5, 114, 122, 129.5, 137]cm)

Materials
Classic Elite Premier; 50% Pima cotton, 50% Tencel; 1¾ oz (50g)/108 yd (99m)

7 (8, 9, 11, 12, 13, 14, 15) hanks in #5275 Coconut (MC)

1 hank in #5216 Natural (CC)

Size I-9 (5.5mm) crochet hook

Size H-9 (5mm) crochet hook for finishing

Gauge
11 BASE CH/SC = 4" (10cm)

In shell pattern, 2 repeats (SH, sc) and 6 rows = 3" (7.5cm)

In sc, worked firmly for finishing, using smaller hook if needed, 12 sc = 4" (10cm)

In sctbl ribbing, using smaller hook, 5 st= 1" (2.5cm), 15 rows = 4" (10cm) unstretched

Arm Band ribbing will stretch to approximately same width as sleeve opening.

Special Stitches
See Jewel, page 37

Sctbl (single crochet through back loop only)

INSTRUCTIONS

This V-neck construction is also used for Rah-boon-dee-ay (page 58). With some modifications, it serves as the basis for the coats Haru (page 110) and Shannon (page 116).

V-NECK YOKE
Shape V-neck front edges at the same time as making the yoke corner increases.

With MC, BASE CH/SC 25 (25, 25, 25, 29, 29, 29) to measure approximately 9 (9, 9, 9, 10½, 10½, 10½)" (23 [23, 23, 23, 26.5, 26.5, 26.5]cm) slightly stretched.

Size 33
Row 1: Ch 1, sc in first sc, [sk next sc, SH in next sc, sk next sc, sc in next sc] 6 times, placing sc in last sc, turn—6 shells.

Row 2 (inc): Ch 4, (dc, ch 1, dc, ch 1, dc) in first sc for corner, *sc in next ch-sp of sh, INC-SH in next sc for corner*, [sc in next ch-sp of sh, SH in next sc] 3 times, repeat from * to * twice, turn—7 pattern repeats.

Row 3 (inc): Ch 1, sc in first dc, sk next ch-sp, INC-SH in corner ch-sp, sc in next ch-sp, *SH in next sc, over inc-sh work (sc in first ch-sp, INC-SH in corner ch-sp, sc in next ch-sp)*, [SH in next sc, sc in next ch-sp of sh] 3 times; repeat from * to * twice, except place last sc in third ch of tch, turn—10 pattern repeats.

Row 4 (inc): Ch 3, 2 dc in first sc, *over inc-sh work (sc in first ch-sp, INC-SH in corner ch-sp, sc in next ch-sp)**, work in pattern to next inc-sh*; repeat from * to * twice, repeat from * to **, ending with 3 dc in last sc. Turn.

Row 5: Ch 1, sc in first dc, SH in next sc, *over inc-sh work (sc in first ch-sp, SH in corner ch-sp, sc in next ch-sp), SH in next sc**, work in pattern to next inc-sh*; repeat from * to *, repeat from * to **, sc in top of tch, turn—18 pattern repeats.

Row 6: Ch 3, (dc, ch 1, 2 dc) in first sc, work in pattern across, placing SH in last sc, turn—19 pattern repeats.

Row 7 (inc): Ch 3, 2 dc in first dc, *work in pattern to next corner sc, INC-SH in corner sc*; repeat from * to * 3 times, work in pattern to end, ending with 3 dc in top of tch, turn.

Row 8: Ch 1, sc in first dc, *work in pattern to next inc-sh, over inc-sh work (sc in first ch-sp, SH in corner ch-sp, sc in next ch-sp)*; repeat from * to * 3 times, work in pattern to end, ending with sc in top of tch, turn—23 pattern repeats.

Row 9–14: Work same as Size 33 Rows 6–8 twice—33 pattern repeats.

Size 36

Row 1–4: Work same as Size 33 Rows 1–4.

Row 5 (inc): Ch 1, sc in first dc, SH in next sc, *over inc-sh work (sc in first ch-sp, INC-SH in corner ch-sp, sc in next ch-sp), SH in next sc**, [sc in next ch-sp of sh, SH in next sc] to next inc-sh*; repeat from * to *, repeat from * to **, sc in top of tch, turn.

Row 6: Ch 3, (dc, ch 1, 2 dc) in first sc, *work in pattern to next inc-sh, over inc-sh work (sc in first ch-sp, SH in corner ch-sp, sc in next ch-sp), SH in next sc*, repeat from * to * 3 times, work in pattern to end, placing SH in last sc, turn.

Row 7: Ch 3, 2 dc in first dc, sc in next ch-sp of sh across, end with 3 dc in top of tch, turn.

Row 8 (inc): Ch 1, sc in first dc, *work in pattern to next corner sc, INC-SH in corner sc*; repeat from * to * 3 times, work in pattern to end, ending with sc in top of tch, turn.

Row 9–15: Repeat Size 36 Rows 6–8 twice, then Row 6 once more—38 pattern repeats.

Size 39

Row 1–5: Same as Size 36 Rows 1–5—18 shells.

Row 6 (inc): Ch 3, (dc, ch 1, 2 dc) in first sc, *work in pattern to next inc-sh, over inc-sh work (sc in first ch-sp, INC-SH in corner ch-sp, sc in next ch-sp)*, repeat from * to * 3 times, work in pattern to end, placing SH in last sc, turn.

Row 7: Ch 3, 2 dc in first dc, *work in pattern to next inc-sh, over inc-sh work (sc in first ch-sp, SH in corner ch-sp, sc in next ch-sp)*; repeat from * to * 3 times, work in pattern to end, ending with 3 dc in top of tch, turn.

Row 8: PATT ROW 1.

Row 9 (inc): Ch 3, (dc, ch 1, 2 dc) in first sc, *work in pattern to next corner sc, INC-SH in corner sc*; repeat from * to * 3 times, work in pattern to end, placing SH in last sc, turn.

Row 10–15: Same as Size 39 Rows 7–9 twice, Size 39 Row 7 once more—38 pattern repeats.

Sizes 42 (45)

Row 1: Work same as Size 33 Row 1.

Along with the 4 principal corners, for next row only inc at center back as follows:

Row 2 (inc): Ch 4, (dc, ch 1, dc, ch 1, dc) in first sc for corner, *sc in next ch-sp of sh, INC-SH in next sc for corner, sc in next ch-sp of sh, SH in next sc*, repeat from * to * twice, sc in next ch-sp of sh, INC-SH in last sc for corner, turn—7 shells.

Row 3 (inc): Ch 1, sc in first dc, sk next ch-sp, INC-SH in corner ch-sp, sc in next ch-sp, *SH in next sc, over inc-sh work (sc in first ch-sp, INC-SH in corner ch-sp, sc in next ch-sp)*, [SH in next sc, sc in next ch-sp of sh], SH in next sc, over center back inc-sh work (sc in first ch-sp, SH in next ch-sp, sc in next ch-sp); repeat between [ ], repeat from * to * twice, except place last sc in third ch of tch, turn—11 shells.

Row 4 (inc): Ch 3, (dc, ch 1, 2 dc) in first sc, *over inc-sh work (sc in first ch-sp, INC-SH in corner ch-sp, sc in next ch-sp)**, work in pattern to next inc-sh*; repeat from * to * twice, repeat from * to **, ending with SH in last sc, turn.

Row 5 (inc): Ch 3, 2 dc in first dc, *work in pattern to next inc-sh, over inc-sh work (sc in first ch-sp, INC-SH in corner ch-sp, sc in next ch-sp)*, repeat from * to * 3 times, sc in next ch-sp of sh, 3 dc in top of tch, turn.

Row 6 (inc): Ch 1, sc in first dc, *work in pattern to next inc-sh, over inc-sh work (sc in first ch-sp, INC-SH in corner ch-sp, sc in next ch-sp)*; repeat from * to * 3 times, work in pattern to end, ending with sc in top of tch, turn.

Row 7–16: Work same as Size 36 Rows 6–8 for 3 times, ROW 6 once more—44 pattern repeats.

Size 48

Row 1–3: Same as Size 33 Rows 1–3 except with an extra repeat at back between corners.

Row 4–6 (inc): Work same as Size 42 Rows 4–6.

Row 7 (inc): Work same as Size 39 Row 6.

Row 8–17 (inc): Work same as Size 39 Rows 7–9 for 3 times, Size 39 Row 7 once more—44 pattern repeats.

Size 51

In first row only inc at center back neck as follows:

Row 1: Ch 1, sc in first sc, [sk next sc, SH in next sc, sk next sc, sc in next sc] 3 times, sk next sc, INC-SH in next sc, sk next sc, sc in next sc, repeat between [ ] 3 times, placing sc in last sc, turn—7 shells.

Row 2 (inc): Ch 4, (dc, ch 1, dc, ch 1, dc) in first sc for corner, sc in next ch-sp of sh, INC-SH in next sc for corner, [sc in next ch-sp of sh, SH in next sc] twice, over inc-sh at center back work (sc in first ch-sp, SH in next ch-sp, sc in next ch-sp), [SH in next sc, sc in next ch-sp of sh] twice, INC-SH in next sc for corner, sc in next ch-sp of sh, INC-SH in last sc, turn—9 shells.

Row 3 (inc): Ch 3, 2 dc in first dc, *over inc-sh work (sc in first ch-sp, INC-SH in corner ch-sp, sc in next ch-sp), SH in next sc*; repeat from * to *, [sc in next ch-sp of sh, SH in next sc] to next inc-sh; repeat from * to * twice, except omit last SH, place last sc in tch sp, end with 3 dc in third ch of tch, turn.

Row 4 (inc): Work same as SIZE 36 ROW 5.

Row 5 (inc): Work same as SIZE 39 ROW 6.

Row 6–7: Work same as Size 42 Rows 5–6.

Row 8–17: Work same as Size 36 Rows 6–8 for 3 times, ROW 6 once more—50 pattern repeats.

Size 54

Row 1–7: Work same as Size 51 Rows 1–7.

Row 8: Work same as Size 39 Row 6.

Row 9–17: Work same as Size 39 Rows 7–9 for 3 times—49 pattern repeats.

Stop here for Haru, continued on page 112, and Shannon, page 118.

JOINING

Sizes join at underarms and front neck at different steps. SIZE 33 joins underarm, then neck. SIZES 36 (42, 45, 51) join underarm and neck in same row. SIZES 39 (48, 54) join neck, then underarm.

Size 33

Join underarm: Ch 3, (dc, ch 1, 2 dc) in first sc, *work in pattern to next corner sh, sc in ch-sp of corner sh, ch 1, BASE CH/SC 7 for underarm, sc in ch-sp of next corner sh*; repeat from * to *, work in pattern, placing SH in last sc, turn.

Sizes 36 (42, 45, 51)

Join underarm and front neck: Ch 3, dc in first dc, *work in pattern to next corner sh, sc in ch-sp of corner sh, ch 1, BASE CH/SC 7 (7, 11, 11) for underarm, sc in ch-sp of next corner sh*; repeat from * to *, work in pattern to end, ending with 2 dc in top of tch, ch 1, sl st in top of beg ch, fasten off.

Sizes 39 (48, 54)

Join front neck: Ch 3, dc in first dc, *work in pattern to next inc-sh, over inc-sh work (sc in first ch-sp, SH in corner ch-sp, sc in next ch-sp)*, repeat from * to * 3 times, work in pattern to end, ending with 2 dc in top of tch, ch 1, sl st in top of beg ch, turn.

Sizes 39 (48, 54)

Join underarm: Ch 1, sc in same ch-sp, *work in pattern to next corner sh, sc in ch-sp of corner sh, ch 1, BASE CH/SC 7 (11, 11) for underarm, sc in ch-sp of next corner sh*; repeat from * to *, work in pattern to end, sl st in beg sc, fasten off.

BODY

Size 33

Join front neck and fill in pattern at underarms as follows.

Rnd 1: Ch 3, dc in first dc, *work in pattern to underarm, placing SH in sc before underarm, sk next 3 sc, sc in next sc, sk remaining 3 sc of underarm, SH in next sc*; repeat from * to *, work in pattern to end, ending with 2 dc in last sc, ch 1, sl st in top of beg ch, fasten off.

All Other Sizes

Sk backward to center of underarm. Now working again toward front, begin working in joined rounds, filling in pattern at underarms.

Sizes 36 (39, 42)

Rnd 1: Join with sl st in 4th sc at center of underarm, ch 1, sc in same sc, *sk remaining 3 sc of underarm, SH in next sc, work in pattern across, placing SH in sc before next underarm, sk next 3 sc, sc in next sc*; repeat from * to *, except omit last sc, instead end with sl st in beg sc, turn.

Sizes 45 (48, 51, 54)

Rnd 1: Join with sl st in 6th sc at center of underarm, ch 3, dc in same sc, *sk next 2 sc, sc in next sc, sk remaining 2 sc, SH in next sc, work in pattern across, placing SH in sc before next underarm, sk next 2 sc, sc in next sc, sk next 2 sc, SH in next sc*; repeat from * to *, except omit last SH, instead work 2 dc in same sc as beg, sc in top of beg ch, turn.
Work one round even on 22 (24, 26, 28, 30, 32, 34, 36) pattern repeats, now working toward back.

Size 33

Rnd 2: Turn, join with sl st in sc at center of next underarm, now working toward back, PATT RND 2.

Sizes 36 (39, 42)

Rnd 2: PATT RND 2.

Sizes 45 (48, 51, 54)
Rnd 2: PATT RND 1.

Adjusting for full bust
Insert bust short rows as for Jewel (page 40) here if desired. **Note:** If you made A and B short rows, ignore the sl sts and work the next round in pattern as facing.
Stop here for Rah-boon-dee-ay, continued on page 60.

HIP SHAPING

For a longer body with more ease in the hip (6" [15cm] extra ease), work this set of increases, beginning just past the waist.
Begin with PATT RND 1 (1, 1, 1, 2, 2, 2, 2), work even in established pattern for 14 (15, 14, 14, 14, 13, 13, 14) rounds, ending with PATT RND 2 (1, 2, 2, 1, 2, 2, 1), approximately 8" (20.5cm) from underarm.

Sizes 33 (39, 42, 48, 51)
Hip Shaping: Ch 1, sc in same ch-sp, *[SH in next sc, sc in next ch-sp of sh] 3 (4, 4, 5, 5) times, INC-SH in next sc, sc in next ch-sp of sh, repeat between [ ] 3 (3, 4, 4, 5) times, INC-SH in next sc, sc in next ch-sp of sh, repeat between [ ] 3 (4, 4, 5, 5) times*; repeat from * to *, except omit last sc, instead end with sl st in beg sc, turn.

Sizes 36 (45, 54)
Hip Shaping: Ch 3, dc in same sc, *[sc in next ch-sp of sh, SH in next sc] 3 (4, 5) times, sc in next ch-sp of sh, INC-SH in next sc*; repeat from * to *, repeat between [ ] 4 (5, 6) times, repeat from * to * twice, repeat between [ ] 3 (4, 5) times, sc in next ch-sp of sh, 2 dc in same sc as beg, sc in top of beg ch, turn.
Next Rnd: Work as PATT RND 2 (1, 2, 2, 1, 2, 2, 1), except over inc-sh work (sc in first ch-sp, SH in next ch-sp, sc in next ch-sp)—26 (28, 30, 32, 34, 36, 38, 40) pattern repeats.
Work even until 30 rounds total from underarm, approximately 15" (38cm) from underarm, or to desired length. Fasten off.

SLEEVES

The sleeves are full-width, elbow length, gently gathered into contrast ribbed bands.
Rnd 1: With MC, make sleeve on armhole the same as Jewel Rnd 1 (page 40)—8 (9, 10, 10, 11, 12, 12, 13) pattern repeats.
Work pattern rounds even until 7–7.5" (18–19cm) from underarm, 14 or 15 rounds total, end by working PATT RND 1, turn.

Adjusting sleeve width
I suggest the larger sizes, 48 (51, 54), taper upper arm once, to 11 (11, 12) pattern repeats, same as Jewel (page 41). 8 (9, 10, 10, 11, 11, 11, 12) pattern repeats. There is no obvious RS or WS until now. All sizes turn, RS now facing, make 5 sc across each pattern repeat, working firmly to gauge of 12 sc = 4" (10cm), switching to smaller hook if needed to achieve gauge.
Next Rnd (RS): Ch 1, sk same sc, [sc in each of next 2 dc, ch-sp, and 2 dc, sk next sc] around, end with sl st in beg sc, fasten off—40 (45, 50, 50, 55, 55, 55, 60) sc.

ARM BAND

With CC and smaller hook, RS facing, join with sl st in same sc, ch 6.
Foundation (RS): Sc in second ch from hook, sc in each of 4 remaining ch, sl st in each of next 2 sc of sleeve, turn—5 sc.
Row 1 (WS): Sk next 2 sl st, sctbl in each of next 5 sc, turn.
Row 2 (RS): Ch 1, sctbl in each of next 5 sc, sl st in each of next 2 sc of sleeve, turn.
Repeat Rows 1–2 around sleeve. SIZES 33 (39, 42, 54) end by sl st in each of last 2 sc of sleeve, repeat Row 1. SIZES 36 (45, 48, 51) omit last sl st of Row 2. All sizes, fasten off, leaving a few inches tail for seaming. Holding last row together with spare loops of foundation chain, matching stitches, whipstitch together through 5 sts, fasten off.
Make second sleeve and arm band in the same way.

FINISHING
V-NECK EDGE

With MC, finish neck edge with a RS round of sc, working firmly to gauge of 12 sc = 4" (10cm), switching to smaller hook if needed to achieve gauge.

V-Neck Edge Rnd 1: RS facing, join with sl st in 13th (13th, 13th, 13th, 13th, 15th, 15th, 15th) base ch at center back of neck, ch 1, sc in same ch, sc in each remaining ch, [sc in each sc row edge, 2 sc in each dc row edge] of V-neck shaping. At point of V, sc in bottom of sc, repeat between [ ] to neck base ch, sc in each remaining ch, sl st in beg sc, fasten off—78 (78, 78, 82, 82, 86, 90, 90) sc.

Mark the sc at the center point of V.

NECK BAND

With CC, make a 1" (2.5cm) wide band of ribbing with a crossover front at the V. The first row of ribbing begins directly on 5 sc of neck, then is worked sideways around the neck. The last rows are made in the spare loops behind the first row.

Row 1 (WS): With CC and smaller hook, WS facing, join with sl st in back lp only of marked center point sc, sk same sc, sctbl in each of next 5 sc, turn—5 sc.

Row 2 (RS): Ch 1, sctbl in each of next 5 sc, sl st in each of next 2 sc of neck, turn.

Row 3 (WS): Sk next 2 sl st, sctbl in each of next 5 sc, turn.

Repeat ROWS 2–3 around all sc of neck until you reach the 5 sc of neck previously worked in ROW 1.

Underlap Row 1: Ch 1, sctbl in each of next 5 sc, working behind previous sc of ROW 1, sl st in each of next 2 spare lps of neck, turn.

Underlap Row 2: Sk next 2 sl st, sctbl in each of next 5 sc, turn.

Repeat UNDERLAP ROWS 1–2, then UNDERLAP 1 once more, ending with sl st in last spare lp, fasten off, leaving few inches tail for sewing. Thread tail on yarn needle. On inside of neckline, sk center point sc, and holding last row together with next 5 sc going up V-neck behind other end of band, matching sts, whip stitch together, fasten off.

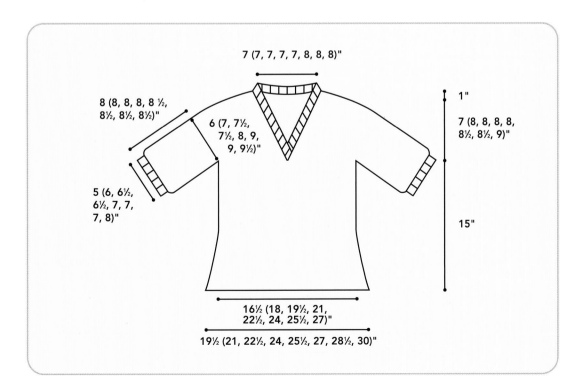

7 (7, 7, 7, 8, 8, 8)"

8 (8, 8, 8, 8½, 8½, 8½, 8½)"

6 (7, 7½, 7½, 8, 9, 9, 9½)"

1"

7 (8, 8, 8, 8, 8½, 8½, 9)"

5 (6, 6½, 6½, 7, 7, 7, 8)"

15"

16½ (18, 19½, 21, 22½, 24, 25½, 27)"

19½ (21, 22½, 24, 25½, 27, 28½, 30)"

RAH-BOON-DEE-AY

Lavish ruffled lace encircles this festive, girly-girl sweater. Designed to be worn over slim pants or a pencil skirt, this variation is not for everyone. If you can pull it off, make this crocheted V-neck pullover with an added deep, flirty lace trim. If you don't want all that froth around your hips, omit the lace around the bottom, finish the sweater at your best length, and just add trim to the sleeves.

Yarn Notes: See how crocheting a finer, silkier yarn to the same gauge creates a much lacier fabric with a looser hand and serious stretch. The stitches are so loose that this top will grow considerably in the lower body and sleeve length when blocked and worn. I have compensated for this effect when calculating the number of rows to crochet for each finished length given. Don't be shocked at how short it looks before blocking. And don't be tempted to add rows unless you really mean it!

R A H -
B O O N -
D E E - A Y

Skill Level	INTERMEDIATE	3 LIGHT

INSTRUCTIONS

Size

Finished bust: 33 (36, 39, 42, 45, 48, 51, 54)" (84 [91, 99, 106.5, 114, 122, 129.5, 137]cm)

Materials

South West Trading Company Pure; 100% soy silk; 1¾ oz (50g)/164 yd (150m)

6 (7, 7, 8, 9, 9, 10, 11) balls in #075 Poinsettia

Size I-9 (5.5mm) crochet hook

Size H-9 (5mm) crochet hook for finishing

Gauge

11 BASE CH/SC = 4" (10cm)

In shell pattern, 2 repeats and 6 rows = 3" (7.5cm) (blocks to 6 rows = approximately 3½" [9cm])

In sc, worked firmly for finishing, using smaller hook if needed, 12 sc = 4" (10cm)

Lace Trim, as crocheted, 5 rnds = 5" (12.5cm) (blocks to 6" [15cm])

Using smaller hook, 3 scallops of neck trim = 2" (5cm)

This gauge is oversized for this weight yarn; keep work relaxed.

Special Stitches

See Jewel, page 37

V: (Dc, ch 3, dc) in same st or sp

CL (cluster): Dc3tog in same st

PICOT: Ch 3, sl st in st just made by: insert hook from top to bottom under 2 forward strands, sl st to close picot.

SCALLOP: (Sl st, ch 2, hdc) all in next st.

YOKE

Same as Tall Latte V-Neck Yoke (page 52) through BODY RND 2. Make bust short rows if desired.

BODY

Work body straight or include Tall Latte Hip Shaping (page 56) if desired, until approximately 11" (28cm) (will block to 13" [33cm]) from underarm, 20 or 21 more rounds, or to desired length before trim. End by working PATT RND 1.

LACE TRIM

Made in joined rounds on any number of shell pattern repeats, continue with same size hook as used for Body. There is no obvious RS or WS so far. All sizes turn, RS now facing.

Rnd 1 (RS): Ch 6 (counts as dc, ch 3), [sc in next ch-sp of sh, ch 3, V in next sc, ch 3] around, except omit last V and ch 3, instead end with dc in same sc as beg, ch 1, hdc in third ch of beg ch.

Rnd 2: Ch 7 (counts as dc, ch 4), [tr in next sc, ch 4, V in next ch-3 sp of V, ch 4] around, except omit last V and ch 4, instead end with dc in same ch-sp as beg, ch 1, hdc in third ch of beg ch.

Rnd 3: Ch 7, sk same ch-sp, [sc in next ch-4 sp, sc in next tr, sc in next ch-4 sp, ch 4, V in next ch-3 sp of V, ch 4] around, except omit last V and ch 4, instead end with dc in same ch-sp as beg, ch 1, hdc in third ch of beg ch.

Rnd 4: Ch 6 (counts as dc, ch 3), dc in same ch-sp, *ch 4, sc in each of next 3 sc, ch 4, (V, ch 3, V) in next ch-3 sp of V*; repeat from * to * around, except end with V in same ch-sp as beg, ch 1, hdc in third ch of beg ch.

Rnd 5: Ch 7, dc in next ch-3 sp of V, *ch 4, sk next sc, sc in next sc, ch 4, sk next ch-4 sp, dc in next ch-3 sp of V, ch 4, V in next ch-3 sp, ch 4, dc in next ch-3 sp*; repeat from * to * around, except end with dc in same ch-sp as beg, ch 1, hdc in third ch of beg ch.

Rnd 6: Ch 2, (dc2tog, PICOT, ch 4, CL, PICOT) in same ch-sp, *ch 4, (CL, PICOT) in next ch-4 sp, ch 4, (sc, ch 3, sc) in next sc, ch 4, sk next ch-4 sp, (CL, PICOT) in next ch-4 sp, (ch 4, CL, PICOT) 3 times in next ch-sp of V*; repeat from * to * around, except end with (ch 4, CL, PICOT) in same ch-sp as beg, ch 4, sl st in top of beg cl, fasten off.

SLEEVES

These sleeves are full-width, half-length before adding lace trim.

Rnd 1: With MC make sleeve on armhole same as Jewel Rnd 1 (page 40)—8 (9, 10, 10, 11, 12, 12, 13) pattern repeats.

Work in pattern rounds even until approximately 6"

(15cm) (blocks to 7" [18cm]) from underarm, 12 or 13 rounds from underarm, or to desired length before trim. End by working PATT RND 1.

Adjusting sleeve width

I suggest Sizes 48, 51, and 54 taper upper arm once, to 11 (11, 12) pattern repeats, same as Jewel (page 41). 8 (9, 10, 10, 11, 11, 11, 12) pattern repeats. With RS facing, as determined by RS of Body, work same Lace Trim Rnds 1–6.

Make second sleeve and lace trim in the same way.

FINISHING
NECK EDGE

Onto the finishing round of sc, make little scallops, switching to smaller hook and working firmly to gauge of 12 sts = 4" (10cm).

Rnd 1 (RS): Same as Tall Latte V-Neck Edge Rnd 1 (page 41), do not fasten off, do not turn—78 (78, 78, 82, 82, 86, 90, 90) sc.

Mark the sc at the center point of V.

Rnd 2 (RS): Ch 2, hdc in same sc, [sk next sc, SCALLOP in next sc] across to 2 sc before center marker, sk next 2 sc, SCALLOP in center sc, sk next 2 sc, SCALLOP in next sc, repeat between [ ] to end, sk last sc, sl st in same sc as beg, fasten off.

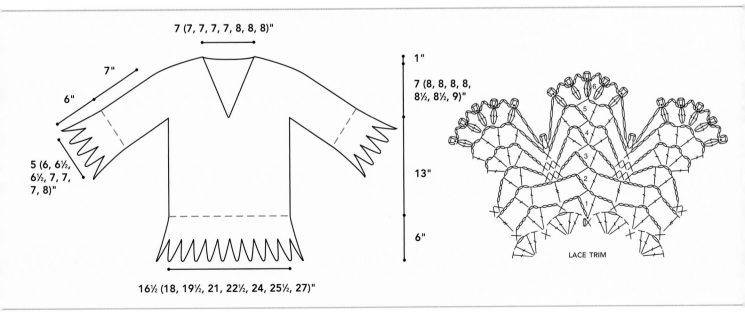

7 (7, 7, 7, 7, 8, 8, 8)"

7"

6"

5 (6, 6½, 6½, 7, 7, 7, 8)"

16½ (18, 19½, 21, 22½, 24, 25½, 27)"

1"

7 (8, 8, 8, 8, 8½, 8½, 9)"

13"

6"

LACE TRIM

|4|
CAPTIVATING COVER-UPS
CARDIGANS

Cardigans are versatile outer layers, and depending on your choice of yarns and colors, can be adapted for year-round wear. The samples in the following group are all crocheted from the same basic design with common elements: a lovely but simple semiopen pattern stitch, seamless construction with raglan-shaped yoke, a rounded neck, and open front. Once you're familiar with the basic design, you'll want to try all of the variations or come up with your own best combination of length, sleeve, and finish.

YARN NOTES

Use medium to heavy worsted weight yarns, ball band symbol 4, generally having a knitting gauge of 4 to 5 sts per 1" (2.5cm) or the equivalent in multiple strands of finer yarns.

SIZE FINDER

Meant to be worn over a light first layer, these cardigans do not need to close completely across the bust, and the fabric is stretchy, so there is a great deal of latitude in fit. Choose the size that is closest to your actual bust, within an inch or two (2.5–5cm) either way.

CINNABAR

With its clean, classic silhouette, this sweater can go anywhere. It features long tapered sleeves, mid-hip length, and wide bands with rope edging. The worsted weight yarn, a tweedy, luxurious wool and silk blend, crocheted in this stitch pattern of shells and Vs, makes a fabric that is lacy but substantial, warm but not stuffily so. Use a clasp, sweater pin, or brooch or add a belt (page 126) or a button link (page 136) to close the front where and when you please.

CINNABAR

Skill Level | INTERMEDIATE | 4 MEDIUM

Size

Finished bust: 35 (40, 45, 50, 55, 60)" (88 [101.5, 114, 127, 140, 152.5]cm), not including bands

Materials

Tahki New Tweed; 60% merino wool, 26% viscose, 14% silk; 1¾ oz (50g)/92 yd (85m)

9 (10, 12, 13, 15, 17) balls in #046 Deep Red

In-Line button link (page 137)

Size J-10 (6mm) crochet hook

Size I-9 (5.5mm) crochet hook for finishing

Gauge

Using larger hook, 10 BASE CH/SC or sc = 4" (10cm)

In Shell and V pattern, one repeat (SH, V) = 2½" (6.5cm), 6 rows in pattern = 4" (10cm)

Using smaller hook, in sc mesh or rev-sc rope of band, 6 repeats (sc, ch 1) = 4" (10cm)

INSTRUCTIONS

YOKE

BASE CH/SC 31 (31, 31, 31, 35, 35) to measure approximately 12 (12, 12, 12, 14, 14)" (30.5 [30.5, 30.5, 30.5, 35.5, 35.5]cm) stretched.

Sizes 35 (40, 45, 50)

Row 1 (inc): Ch 4 (counts as dc, ch 1), (dc, ch 1, V) in first sc for corner, sk next 2 sc, SH in next sc, sk next 2 sc, INC-V in next sc for corner, sk next 2 sc, SH in next sc, [sk next 2 sc, V in next sc, sk next 2 sc, SH in next sc] twice, sk next 2 sc, INC-V in next sc for corner, sk next 2 sc, SH in next sc, sk next 2 sc, INC-V in last sc for corner, turn—5 shells.

Sizes 55 (60)

For a larger neckline, cheat 2 extra stitches by making an increase at the center back neck as follows:

Row 1 (inc): Ch 4 (counts as dc, ch 1), (dc, ch 1, V) in first sc for corner, sk next 2 sc, [SH in next sc, sk next 2 sc, INC-V in next sc for corner, sk next 2 sc, SH in next sc], sk next sc, V in next sc, sk next 2 sc, SH in next sc, sk next 2 sc, INC-V in next sc for corner, sk next 2 sc, SH in next sc, sk next 2 sc, V in next sc, sk next sc, repeat between [ ] once, sk next 2 sc, INC-V in last sc for corner, turn—6 shells.

Size 35

Row 2: Ch 3, (dc, ch 1, 2 dc) in first V, V in corner ch-sp, SH in V, *[V in shell, SH in V] to next corner ch-sp, V in

Special Stitches

SH: (2 dc, ch 1, 2 dc) all in same st or sp.

V: (dc, ch 1, dc) all in same st or sp.

INC-V: (V, ch 1, V) all in same st or sp.

INC-V

SH in V: Make a shell in the ch-1 sp of next V.

V in shell: Make a V in the ch-1 sp of next shell.

Rev sc: Working backward, from left to right, insert hook in next st to the right, make sc.

Stitch Pattern Notes

This pattern uses a variation of Shell and V. Except for the ends of rows or where there's any shaping, you will always make a shell in a V and a V in a shell.

STITCH PATTERN (IN ROWS, FOR YOKE AND BODY)

PATT ROW 1: Ch 3, dc in first dc, [SH in V, V in shell] across, except omit last V, instead end with 2 dc in top of tch, turn.

PATT ROW 2: Ch 3, 2 dc in first dc, [V in shell, SH in V] across, except omit last SH, instead end with 3 dc in top of tch, turn.

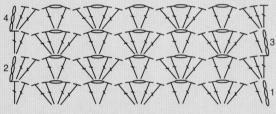

STITCH PATTERN IN ROWS

YOKE STITCH PATTERN (FOR YOKE INCREASES, IN ROUNDS)

YOKE 1 (inc) (as PATT ROW 1): Ch 3, dc in first dc, *work in pattern to next corner ch-sp, INC-V in next corner ch-sp*; repeat from * to * 3 more times, work in pattern to end, ending with 2 dc in top of tch, turn.

YOKE 2 (even) (as PATT ROW 2): Ch 3, 2 dc in first dc, *work in pattern to next corner ch-sp, V in next corner ch-sp*; repeat from * to * 3 more times, work in pattern to end, ending with

3 dc in top of tch, turn.

YOKE 3 (inc) (as PATT ROW 2): Ch 3, 2 dc in first dc, *work in pattern to next corner ch-sp, INC-V in next corner ch-sp*; repeat from * to * 3 more times, work in pattern to end, ending with 3 dc in top of tch, turn.

YOKE 4 (even) (as PATT ROW 1): Ch 3, dc in first dc, *work in pattern to next corner ch-sp, V in next corner ch-sp*; repeat from * to * 3 more times, work in pattern to end, ending with 2 dc in top of tch, turn.

STITCH PATTERN (FOR SLEEVES, IN ROUNDS)

PATT RND 1: Ch 3, dc in first ch-sp, [V in shell, SH in V] around, except omit last SH, instead end with 2 dc in same ch-sp as beg, sc in top of beg ch, turn.

PATT RND 2: Ch 3, [SH in V, V in shell] around, except omit last V, instead end with dc in same sp as beg, sc in top of beg ch, turn.

TAPER PATTERN (FOR TAPERING SLEEVES, IN ROUNDS)

To decrease sts, convert a shell to a V over 3 rounds.

TAPER RND 1: Ch 3, [V in shell, SH in V] around, except omit last SH, instead end with dc in same ch-sp as beg, sc in top of beg ch, turn.

TAPER RND 2: Ch 3, (dc, ch 1, 2 dc) for dec in next V, [V in shell, SH in V] around, except omit last SH, instead (2 dc, ch 1, dc) for dec in last V, dc in same ch-sp as beg, sc in top of beg ch, turn.

TAPER RND 3: Ch 3, V in next ch-sp, [SH in V, V in shell] around, placing last V in ch-sp of dec shell, dc in same ch-sp as beg, sc in top of beg ch, turn—one less shell.

Mark the Vs on either side of the beginning V. Move markers out as you convert more shells as indicated:

TAPER RND 4: Ch 3, V in each V to marked V, V in marked V, [V in shell, SH in V] to marked V, omit SH, instead V in marked V, V in each V to end, dc in same ch-sp as beg, sc in top of beg ch, turn. Move markers out to next V on each side.

TAPER RND 5: Ch 3, V in each V to marked V, (dc, ch 1, 2 dc) in marked V, [V in shell, SH in V] to marked V, omit SH, instead (2 dc, ch 1, dc) in marked V, V in each V to end, dc in same ch-sp as beg, sc in top of beg ch, turn.

TAPER RND 6: Ch 3, V in each V to marker, V in marked dec shell, [SH in V, V in shell] to marker, placing V in marked dec shell, V in each V to end, dc in same ch-sp as beg, sc in top of beg ch, turn—one less shell.

corner ch-sp, SH in V*; repeat from * to * 3 times, except omit last SH, instead (2 dc, ch 1, dc) in tch-sp, dc in third ch of tch, turn—10 pattern repeats.

Row 3: PATT ROW 2, fasten off, turn.

Add sts to shape front neck, increase corners as follows:

Row 4 (inc): BASE CH/SC 6 (for front neck extension),

V in first dc, SH in V, INC-V in next corner ch-sp, SH in V, V in shell, SH in V, INC-V in next corner ch-sp, SH in V, [V in shell, SH in V] to next corner ch-sp, INC-V in next corner ch-sp, SH in V, V in top of tch, ch 1, BASE CH/SC 6 (for front neck extension), turn.

Row 5 (even): Ch 3, 2 dc in first sc of base ch, sk next 2 sc, V in next sc, sk remaining 2 sc, *SH in V, [V in shell, SH in V] to next corner ch-sp, V in corner ch-sp*; repeat from * to * 3 times, SH in V, V in shell, SH in last V, sk next 2 sc of base ch, V in next sc, sk next 2 sc, 3 dc in last sc, turn.

Row 6–10: PATT ROW 1, YOKE 3–4, PATT ROW 2, PATT ROW 1 once more—16 pattern repeats.

Size 40

Row 2 (inc): Ch 3, (dc, ch 1, 2 dc) in first V, INC-V in corner ch-sp, SH in V, * [V in shell, SH in V] to next corner ch-sp, INC-V in corner ch-sp, SH in V*; repeat from * to * 3 times, except omit last SH, instead end (2 dc, ch 1, dc) in tch-sp, dc in third ch of tch, turn—10 shells.

Row 3 (even): Ch 3, 2 dc in first dc, *[V in shell, SH in V] to next corner ch-sp, V in corner ch-sp, SH in V*; repeat from * to * 3 times, V in shell, 3 dc in top of tch, fasten off, turn.

Add sts to shape front neck, work corners even as follows.

Row 4 (even): BASE CH/SC 6 (for front neck extension), V in first dc, SH in V, [V in shell, SH in V] across, end with V in top of tch, ch 1, BASE CH/SC 6 (for front neck extension), turn.

Row 5 (inc): Ch 3, 2 dc in first sc of base ch, sk next 2 sc, V in next sc, sk remaining sc, SH in V, *[V in shell,

SH in V] to next corner ch-sp, INC-V in corner ch-sp, SH in V*; repeat from * to * 3 times, repeat between [ ], sk next 2 sc of base ch, V in next sc, sk next 2 sc, 3 dc in last sc, turn—16 pattern repeats.

Row 6–11: YOKE 4, PATT ROW 2, YOKE 1–2, PATT ROW 1–2—24 pattern repeats.

Size 45

Inc at four corners and at center back neck as follows.

Row 2 (inc): Ch 3, (dc, ch 1, 2 dc) in first V, INC-V in corner ch-sp, SH in V, *[V in shell, SH in V] to next corner ch-sp, INC-V in corner ch-sp, SH in V*, V in shell, SH in V, INC-V in shell at center back, SH in V; repeat from * to * twice, except omit last SH, instead (2 dc, ch 1, dc) in tch-sp, dc in third ch of tch, turn—10 shells.

Row 3 (even): Ch 3, 2 dc in first dc, *[V in shell, SH in V] to next corner ch-sp, V in corner ch-sp, SH in V*; repeat from * to * 4 times, V in shell, 3 dc in top of tch, fasten off, turn.

Add sts to shape front neck as follows.

Row 4 (even): Same as Size 40 Row 4.

Inc across front neck to balance center back, inc at 4 corners as follows.

Row 5 (inc): Ch 3, dc in first sc of base ch, sk next sc, SH in next sc, sk next 2 sc, V in remaining sc, SH in V, *[V in shell, SH in V] to next corner ch-sp, INC-V in corner ch-sp, SH in V*; repeat from * to * 3 times, repeat between [ ], V in first sc of base ch, sk next 2 sc, SH in next sc, sk next sc, 2 dc in last sc, turn—18 pattern repeats.

Row 6–11: YOKE 2, PATT ROW 1, YOKE 3–4, PATT ROW 2, then PATT ROW 1 once more—26 pattern repeats.

Size 50

Row 2–11: Same as Size 45 Rows 2–11.
Row 12: PATT ROW 2—26 pattern repeats.

Size 55

Work even over center back inc, inc 4 principal corners as follows:

Row 2 (inc): Ch 3, (dc, ch 1, 2 dc) in first V, INC-V in

corner ch-sp, SH in V, *[V in shell, SH in V] to next corner ch-sp, INC-V in corner ch-sp, SH in V*, [V in shell, SH in V] to center back corner ch-sp, V in center ch-sp, SH in V; repeat from * to * twice, except omit last shell, instead (2 dc, ch 1, dc) in tch-sp, dc in third ch of tch, turn—12 pattern repeats.

Row 3 (even): Ch 3, 2 dc in first dc, *[V in shell, SH in V] to next corner ch-sp, V in corner ch-sp, SH in V*; repeat from * to * 3 times, V in shell, 3 dc in top of tch, turn.

Row 4 (even): Ch 4, dc in first dc, [SH in V, V in shell] across, ending with V in top of tch, fasten off, turn—16 pattern repeats.

Add sts to shape front neck, inc corners as follows:

Row 5 (inc): BASE CH/SC 8 (for front neck extension), dc in first dc, (dc, ch 1, 2 dc) in next ch-sp, *[V in shell, SH in V] to next corner ch-sp, INC-V in corner ch-sp, SH in V*; repeat from * to * 3 times, V in shell, (2 dc, ch 1, dc) in last V, dc in third ch of tch, ch 1, BASE CH/SC 8 (for front neck extension), turn.

Row 6 (even): Ch 3, dc in first sc, sk next sc, SH in next sc, sk next 2 sc, V in next sc, sk next sc, SH in remaining sc, *[V in shell, SH in V] to next corner ch-sp, V in corner ch-sp, SH in V*; repeat from * to * 3 times, repeat between [ ], V in last shell, SH in first sc of base ch, sk next sc, V in next sc, sk next 2 sc, SH in next sc, sk next sc, 2 dc in last sc, turn—24 shells.

Row 7–12: PATT ROW 2, YOKE 1–2, PATT ROW 1–2, PATT ROW 1 once more—28 pattern repeats.

Size 60

Row 2–6: Same as Size 55 Rows 2–6—24 pattern repeats.

Row 7–13: PATT ROW 2, YOKE 1–2, then PATT ROW 1–2 twice—32 pattern repeats.

JOINING

SIZES 35 (40, 45) have a V at each corner; SIZES 50 (55, 60) have a shell at each corner. Leave corner markers in the ch-sp at corners for later use. Join fronts and back with additional sts at each underarm.

Sizes 35 (40, 45)

Begin as PATT ROW 2 (1, 2): *work in pattern, placing SH in next corner V, ch 1, BASE CH/SC 5 for underarm, SH in next corner V*; repeat from * to *, work in pattern to end, ending as PATT ROW 2 (1, 2), turn.

Sizes 50 (55, 60)

Join Row: Begin as PATT ROW 1 (2, 1): *work in pattern, placing V in next corner shell, ch 1, BASE CH/SC 11 for underarm, V in next corner shell*; repeat from * to *, work in pattern to end, ending as PATT ROW 1 (2, 1), turn.

BODY

Fill in stitch pattern across underarms as follows:

Sizes 35 (40, 45)

Row 1: Begin as PATT ROW 1 (2, 1): *work in pattern to underarm base ch, sk next 2 sc of underarm, SH in next sc, sk remaining 2 sc of underarm, V in shell*; repeat from * to *, work in pattern to end, ending as PATT ROW 1 (2, 1), turn—14 (16, 18) pattern repeats.

Sizes 50 (55, 60)

Row 1: Begin as PATT ROW 2 (1, 2): *work in pattern to underarm, sk next 2 sc of underarm, V in next sc, sk next 2 sc, SH in next sc, sk next 2 sc, V in next sc, sk remaining 2 sc, SH in V*; repeat from * to *, work in pattern to end, ending as PATT ROW 2 (1, 2), turn—20 (22, 24) pattern repeats, with a shell at center of underarm.

All Sizes

Row 2: Work PATT ROW 2 (1, 2, 1, 2, 1).

Adjusting for full bust

Matching short rows are worked on each side of fronts. Mark the V at the center of each underarm.

First Side Short Rows

Begin as PATT ROW 1 (2, 1, 2, 1, 2): work in pattern to shell before marked V at center of underarm, sl st in ch-sp of shell, turn. Sl st in each of next 2 dc and ch-sp of shell, SH in next V, work in pattern to end, ending as PATT ROW 2 (1, 2, 1, 2, 1).

Put the loop on the hook on hold.

Second Side Short Rows

Sk to other underarm.

Join new yarn with sl st in next SH past marked V at center of other underarm, SH in next V, work in pattern to end, ending as PATT ROW 1 (2, 1, 2, 1, 2), turn. Begin as PATT ROW 2 (1, 2, 1, 2, 1), work in pattern to last shell of short row, sl st in ch-sp of shell, fasten off.

Pick up loop on hold, and continue below.

Stop here for Soft Serve, continued on page 74, Mocha Roca, page 78, and Mei-Mei, page 84.

BODY CONTINUED

Note: If you made the bust short rows, when working next row ignore the sl sts of turning and make pattern in sts as facing.

Beginning as PATT ROW 1 (2, 1, 2, 1, 2), work even on 14 (16, 18, 20, 22, 24) pattern repeats for 15 (15, 15, 15, 16, 16) more rows.

Adjusting length

Body is approximately 11 (11, 11, 11, 12, 12)" (28 [28, 28, 28, 30.5, 30.5]cm) from underarm. Band will add 1" (2.5cm) length; blocking will add another 1" (2.5cm). For Petite or a shorter body, omit 2 rows (1½" [3.8cm]). For Tall or a longer body, add 2 rows (1½" [3.8cm]).

CARDIGAN BAND

Band is crocheted in a firmer gauge, 12 sts = 4" (10cm). If you can crochet just a bit tighter using the same larger hook, then continue with it. If not, switch to smaller hook for the band. There is no obvious RS or WS until now. Turn, RS now facing, work sc evenly around entire edge of cardigan as follows.

Rnd 1 (RS): Ch 1, sc in first dc, sc in each dc and ch-sp across lower edge, making a corner of 3 sc in top of tch at end of row, mark middle (second) sc for corner. Rotate and work along row edges of right front, make

2 sc in each dc row edge to front neck base ch, 3 sc in first base ch for corner, mark middle (second) sc for corner, sc in remaining base ch of front neck, 2 sc in each dc row edge to back neck base ch, sc in each base ch of neck, 2 sc in each dc row edge of neck shaping to front neck base ch, sc in next 5 (5, 5, 5, 7, 7) base ch of front neck, 3 sc in last base ch, mark middle (second) sc for corner, 2 sc in each dc row edge down left front; end with 2 sc in top of same dc as beg for corner, sl st in beg sc, turn. Exact count is not critical, but there should always be an odd number. This should adjust itself at the corners.

Rnd 2 (WS): Ch 1, sc in same sc, *[ch 1, sk next sc, sc in next sc] across to corner marker, ch 1, (sc, ch 1, sc) in marked corner sc, move marker into corner ch-sp* repeat from * to * 3 more times, except at end omit (sc, ch 1, sc) in last corner, instead end with sc in same sc as beg, ch 1 for corner ch-sp, sl st in beg sc, turn.

Rnd 3: Ch 1, *[sc in next ch-sp, ch 1] to next corner marker, (sc, ch 1, sc) in marked corner ch-sp, move marker into corner ch-sp, ch 1*; repeat from * to * 3 more times, except end with sc in same corner ch-sp as beg, ch 1, sl st in beg sc, turn.

Rnd 4: Repeat Rnd 3.

Rnd 5 (RS): Ch 1, working backward from left to right [rev sc in next ch-sp, ch 1] around, end with sl st in same ch-sp as beg, fasten off.

SLEEVES

Sleeves are made in joined rounds, back and forth. Taper the sleeve by gradually changing shells into Vs at regular intervals, maintaining repeat count. Convert one shell every three rounds. By the end of the sleeve, there will be 10 (12, 13, 14, 14, 16) Vs. Work sleeves in opposite direction of armhole sts, whether RS or WS for your size.

Sizes 35 (40, 45)

Rnd 1: With appropriate side facing, using larger hook, join yarn with sl st in third ch of underarm, ch 3, sk remaining 2 ch, (2 dc in next dc row edge of shell at join, ch 1, 2 dc in marked corner ch-sp of V) for shell, [V in shell, SH in V] 3 (4, 4) times, V in shell, (2 dc in marked corner ch-sp of V, ch 1, 2 dc in next dc row edge of shell at join) for shell, sk next 2 ch, end with dc in same ch as beg, sc in top of beg ch, turn—5 (6, 6) pattern repeats.

Sizes 50 (55, 60)

Rnd 1: Using larger hook, join yarn with sl st in 6th ch of underarm, ch 3, sk next 2 ch of underarm, SH in next ch, sk remaining 2 ch, (dc in next dc row edge of V at join, ch 1, dc in corner ch-sp of shell) for V, [SH in V, V in shell] 4 (4, 5) times, SH in V, (dc in marked corner ch-sp of shell, ch 1, dc in dc row edge of V at other side of join) for V, sk next 2 ch of underarm, SH in next ch, sk remaining 2 ch, dc in same ch as beg, sc in top of beg ch, turn—7 (7, 8) repeats.

Adjusting sleeves for length

Sleeves will tend to lengthen and skinny out when blocked. Keep this in mind before deciding to adjust sleeves! For Petite or shorter sleeves, SIZES 35 (40, 45, 50, 55), omit 2 rounds (1½" [3.8cm]) or more before taper begins, ending with PATT RND 2; SIZE 60, omit last repeat of TAPER RNDS 4–6. Work NEXT RND as below, then work even rounds of Vs to desired length. For Tall or longer sleeves, all sizes add 2 rounds (1½" [3.8cm]) or more before taper begins, ending with PATT RND 2.

SLEEVES CONTINUED

Beginning with PATT RND 1, work 8 (6, 6, 2, 2, 0) rounds even, then work TAPER RNDS 1–6, then TAPER RNDS 4–6 for 2 (3, 3, 4, 4, 5) times—1 shell remaining.

Next Rnd: Ch 3, V in each V and remaining shell, dc in same ch-sp as beg, sc in top of beg ch.

Sizes 50 (55)

Next Rnd: Ch 3, V in each V, dc in same sp as beg, sc in top of beg ch, turn 10 (12, 12, 14, 14, 16) Vs.

SLEEVE BANDS

Work to a gauge of 11 sc = 4" (10cm), switching to smaller hook if needed. Begin with RS facing (as determined by body band).

Rnd 1 (RS): Ch 1, sc in first ch-sp, sc in each dc and ch-sp of V around, sl st in beg sc, turn—30 (36, 36, 42, 42, 48) sc.

Rnd 2: Ch 1, [sc in next sc, ch 1, sk next sc] 15 (18, 18, 21, 21, 24) times, sl st in beg sc, turn.

Rnd 3: Ch 1, [sc in next ch-sp, ch 1] 15 (18, 18, 21, 21, 24) times, sl st in beg sc, turn.

Rnd 4: Repeat Rnd 3.

Rnd 5 (RS): Ch 1, working backward from left to right [rev sc in next ch-sp, ch 1] 15 (18, 18, 21, 21, 24) times, sl st in same sp as beg, fasten off.

Make second sleeve in the same way.

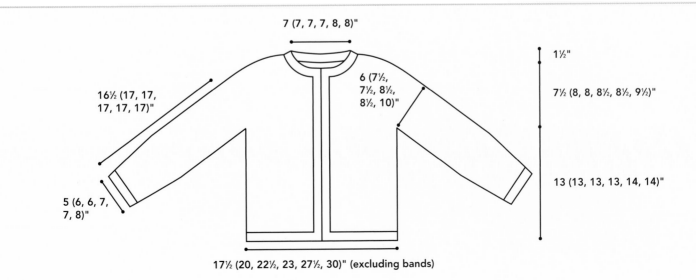

7 (7, 7, 7, 8, 8)"

16½ (17, 17, 17, 17, 17)"

6 (7½, 7½, 8½, 8½, 10)"

1½"

7½ (8, 8, 8½, 8½, 9½)"

5 (6, 6, 7, 7, 8)"

13 (13, 13, 13, 14, 14)"

17½ (20, 22½, 23, 27½, 30)" (excluding bands)

SOFT SERVE

This is a shortie cardigan as bed jacket with a modern, relaxed feel. For lounging comfort, it is cropped so you're not constantly sitting on the back of it, with half-length sleeves that won't drag in your breakfast tray and a more open neckline with string ties for easy on, easy off. The bottom edge and sleeves are slightly flared and trimmed with scallops. The sample is shown in dense, satiny yarn made of bamboo with a sinfully luscious hand—swingy and sweet over a nightgown. But you could crochet it in a dressier yarn for an evening jacket, or in a wooly yarn to wear with jeans. By the way, this would make a wonderful gift for a loved one who is bedridden or chairbound.

SOFT SERVE

Skill Level | **INTERMEDIATE** | 4 MEDIUM

Size

Finished bust: 35 (40, 45, 50, 55, 60)" (88 [101.5, 114, 127, 140, 152.5]cm), not including bands

Materials

South West Trading Company Twizé; 100% bamboo; 3½ oz (100 g)/120 yd (110 m)

5 (5, 6, 6, 7, 7) skeins in #325 Twue

Size J-10 (6 mm) crochet hook

Size I-9 (5.5 mm) crochet hook for finishing

Gauge

Using J-10 (6 mm) or larger hook, 10 BASE CH/SC or sc = 4" (10cm)

In Shell and V pattern, one repeat (SH, V) = 2½" (6.5cm), 6 rows in pattern = 4" (10cm)

In sc of finishing, 11 sc = 4" (10cm)

Special Stitches

See Cinnabar, page 67

INSTRUCTIONS

This jacket is built on the same pattern as Cinnabar (page 64), with a shorter length, full-width half sleeves, scallop edging, and string ties.

YOKE

Make same as Cinnabar (page 66) through Body Row 2. Make bust short rows if desired.

BODY

Beginning with PATT ROW 1 (2, 1, 2, 1, 2), work even on 14 (16, 18, 20, 22, 24) pattern repeats for 10 (11, 10, 11, 10, 11) more rows, or to desired length. End by working PATT ROW 2.

Adjusting for length

Omit rows here for a shorter jacket, and end by working PATT ROW 2. Add rows here for a longer jacket, and end by working PATT ROW 2.

BODY TRIM

Scallop edging should be worked to gauge with larger hook. Then switch to smaller hook if needed to work sc edge more firmly, to achieve a gauge of 11 sc = 4" (10cm). Turn, all sizes RS now facing, make scallop edging, finishing and string ties in one as follows.

Trim Rnd: Ch 1, sc in first dc, *ch 1, make a SCALLOP of [dc, (ch 1, dc) 4 times] in next V, ch 1, sc in ch-sp of next shell*; repeat from * to * to end, except end with 2 sc in top of tch, rotate, change to smaller hook if needed, and work along row edges of right front, make 2 sc in each dc row edge up right front.

For TIE (approximately 12" (30.5cm) long): *2 sc in next base ch at front neck, ch 50, sl st in second ch from hook, sl st in remaining 48 ch, sl st in top of last sc made, sc in same base ch of neck*, sc in each of 5 (5, 5, 5, 7, 7) remaining base ch, 2 sc in each dc row edge of neck shaping, sc in each base ch of back neck, 2 sc in each dc row edge of neck shaping, sc in next 5 (5, 5, 5, 7, 7) base ch at front neck, repeat from * to * for other TIE, 2 sc in each dc row edge down left front, end with sc in same dc as beg, sl st in beg sc, fasten off.

SLEEVES

Make sleeves on armholes in the same way as Cinnabar as follows.

Rnd 1: Same as Cinnabar Rnd 1 (page 70).
Rnd 2–10: Repeat PATT RND 1–2 for 4 times, then PATT RND 1 once more.

Adjusting sleeve length

This version is a full-width, flared sleeve that hits just at the elbow. Adjust for length before scallop edging. For shorter sleeve, omit rounds, and end by working PATT RND 1. For longer sleeve, add rounds, and end by working PATT RND 1.

SLEEVE TRIM

With RS facing (as determined by body trim), finish sleeve with scallop trim as follows:
Trim Rnd (RS): Ch 1, sc in first ch-sp, *ch 1, make a SCALLOP of [dc, (ch 1, dc) 4 times] in ch-sp of next V, ch 1, sc in ch-sp of next shell*; repeat from * to * to end, except omit last sc, instead sl st in beg sc, fasten off.
Make second sleeve in the same way.

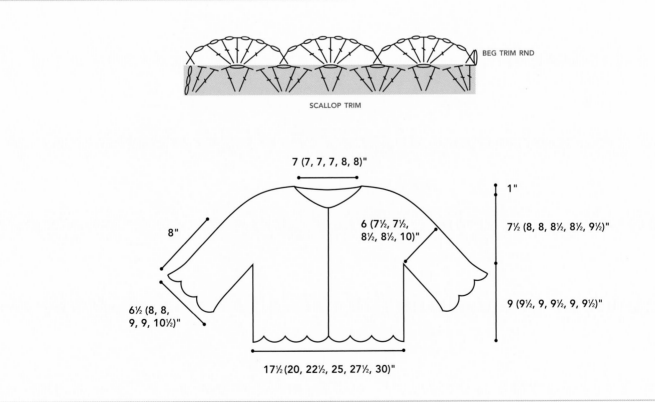

BEG TRIM RND

SCALLOP TRIM

7 (7, 7, 7, 8, 8)"

1"

8"

6 (7½, 7½, 8½, 8½, 10)"

7½ (8, 8, 8½, 8½, 9½)"

6½ (8, 8, 9, 9, 10½)"

9 (9½, 9, 9½, 9, 9½)"

17½ (20, 22½, 25, 27½, 30)"

MOCHA ROCA

A bit of bolero shaping and a wrap-around contrast band turns the Cinnabar cardigan (page 64) into this striking jacket. The wrist-length sleeves are full and slightly flared, cuffed with the same band. The sample is crocheted in three shades of a luxurious blend of wool, cashmere, and angora that's perfect for fall but lightweight enough for year-round wear, in a relaxed fit.

MOCHA ROCA

Skill Level	INTERMEDIATE	4 MEDIUM

Size

Finished bust: 35 (40, 45, 50, 55, 60)" (88 [101.5, 114, 127, 140, 152.5]cm), not including bands

Materials

Classic Elite Princess; 40% merino wool, 28% viscose, 10% cashmere, 7% angora, 15% nylon; 1¾ oz (50g)/150 yd (137m)

4 (5, 5, 6, 7, 7) balls in #3438 Noble Nutmeg (A)

1 (1, 2, 2, 2, 2) balls in #3476 Baronet's Brown (B)

1 (1, 2, 2, 2, 2) balls in #3475 Beyond Beige (C)

Size J-10 (6mm) crochet hook

Size I-9 (5.5mm) crochet hook for finishing

Gauge

Using J-10 (6 mm) or larger hook, 10 BASE CH/SC or sc = 4" (10cm)

In Shell and V pattern, one repeat (SH, V) = 2½" (6.5cm), 6 rows in pattern = 4" (10cm)

Using I-9 (5.5 mm) (or smaller hook), in band, 12 sts = 4" (10cm)

Special Stitches

See Cinnabar, page 67

INSTRUCTIONS

YOKE

With A and the larger hook, make in the same way as Cinnabar (page 66) through Body Row 2. Make bust short rows if desired.

BODY

Beginning with PATT ROW 1 (2, 1, 2, 1, 2), work even on 14 (16, 18, 20, 22, 24) pattern repeats for 5 (6, 7, 6, 7, 8) rows, or for desired length of body before bolero shaping. End with PATT ROW 1.

Adjusting for length

For Petite or a shorter jacket, omit 2 rows (1½" [3.8cm]) or more, ending with PATT ROW 1. For Tall or a longer jacket, add 2 rows (1½" [3.8cm]) or more, ending with PATT ROW 1.

BOLERO SHAPING

Row 1: Ch 3, V in first sh, [SH in V, V in sh] across, V in last sh, dc in top of tch, turn.

Row 2: Sk first dc, sl st in next dc and ch-sp of V, ch 3, V in next sh, [SH in V, V in sh] across, placing V in last sh, dc in last V, turn.

Row 3–4: Repeat Row 2 twice, turn, cont with Body Band—10 (12, 14, 16, 18, 20) pattern repeats.

BODY BAND

Band is crocheted in a firmer gauge of 12 sts = 4" (10cm). Switch to smaller hook. There is no obvious RS or WS until now. Turn, RS now facing. Continuing with A, work sc evenly around entire edge of cardigan.

Note: Mark the stitch at the middle of each of the 2 front neck corners and move or wrap markers up as you go.

Rnd 1 (RS): With A, ch 1, sk first dc, sc in each dc and ch-sp across lower edge to tch. Across bolero shaping make 4 sc in next dc row edge, [sc in ch-sp of V at base of dc edge, 4 sc in next dc row edge] 3 times. Up right-hand front make 2 sc in each dc row edge to front neck base ch, 3 sc in first base ch for corner, mark middle (second) sc for corner, sc in each remaining base ch of front neck, 2 sc in each dc row edge to back neck base ch, sc in each base ch of back neck, 2 sc in each dc row edge to front neck base ch, sc in next 5 (5, 5, 5, 7, 7) base ch of front neck, 3 sc in last base ch, mark middle (second) sc for corner, sc down left-hand front and bolero shaping to correspond with other front, sl st in beg sc, fasten off A—multiple of 4 sc. With RS still facing, locate the sc at dead center of back neck. SIZES 35 (40, 45, 50): Begin next round in same sc. SIZES 55 (60): Sk sc at center back neck, sk next sc, join yarn in next sc.

Rnd 2 (RS): Join B with sl st in designated sc, ch 1, *sc in each sc to marked front neck corner, 3 sc in corner sc*; repeat from * to *, ending sc in each sc to end, sl st in beg sc, fasten off B, turn.

Rnd 3 (WS): Join C with sl st in same sc at center back neck, ch 1, sc in same sc, sk next sc, make a sh of 3 dc in next sc, *[sk next sc, sc in next sc, sk next sc, 3 dc in next sc] to marked corner, sc in corner sc, 3 dc in next sc*; repeat from * to * once, repeat between [ ] to last sc, end with sk last sc, sl st in beg sc, fasten off C, turn.

Rnd 4 (RS): Join B with sl st in same sc, ch 3, dc in same sc, sc in second dc of next sh, *[3 dc in next sc, sc in second dc of next sh] to marked corner sc, 5 dc in corner sc, sc in second dc of next sh*; repeat from *

to *, repeat between [ ] to end, end with dc in same sc as beg, sl st in top of beg ch, fasten off B, turn.

Rnd 5 (WS): Join C in same st, ch 1, sc in same st, 3 dc in next sc, [sc in second dc of next sh, 3 dc in next sc] to 5-dc sh at corner, over corner work (sc in second dc, 3 dc in third dc, sc in 4th dc), 3 dc in next sc*; repeat from * to *, repeat between [ ] to end, end with sl st in beg sc, fasten off C, turn.

Rnd 6 (RS): Join B in same sc, ch 1, sc in same sc, *sc in each dc and sc to marked corner dc, 3 sc in corner dc*, sc in each dc and sc to curve of bolero shaping, [2 sc in next sc, sc in each of next 3 dc] 5 times along bolero curve, repeat from * to *, sc in each dc and sc to end, sl st in beg sc, fasten off B.

SLEEVES

Make sleeves on armholes in the same way as Cinnabar, then work full-width.

Rnd 1: Same as Cinnabar Rnd 1 (page 70).

Rnd 2–15: Repeat PATT RNDS 1–2 for 7 times, then continue with Band—5 (6, 6, 7, 7, 8) pattern repeats.

Adjusting sleeve length

For Petite or shorter sleeves, omit 2 rounds (1½" [3.8cm]) or more. For Tall or longer sleeves, add 2 rounds (1½" [3.8cm]) or more.

SLEEVE BAND

With RS facing (as determined by Body Band), continue with A, switching to smaller hook if needed to work gauge of 12 st = 4" (10cm).

Rnd 1 (RS): Ch 1, sc in same ch-sp, sc in each ch-sp and dc around, sl st in beg sc, fasten off A—40 (48, 48, 56, 56, 64) sc.

Rnd 2 (RS): With RS facing, join B in same sc, ch 1, sc in each sc around, sl st in beg sc, fasten off B, turn.

Rnd 3 (WS): With WS facing, join C in same sc, ch 1, sc in same sc, [sk next sc, 3 dc in next sc, sk next sc, sc in next sc] around, except omit last sc, instead end with sl st in beg sc, fasten off C, turn.

Rnd 4 (RS): With RS facing, join B in same sc, ch 3, dc in same sc, [sc in second dc of next shell, 3 dc in next sc] around, except omit last 3 dc, instead end with dc in same sc as beg, sl st in top of beg ch, fasten off B, turn.

Rnd 5 (WS): Join C in same st, ch 1, sc in same st, [3 dc in next sc, sc in second dc of next shell] around, except omit last sc, instead end sl st in beg sc, fasten off C, turn.

Rnd 6 (RS): With WS facing, join B in same sc, ch 1, sc in same sc, sc in each dc and sc around, sl st in beg sc, fasten off B.

Make second sleeve in the same way.

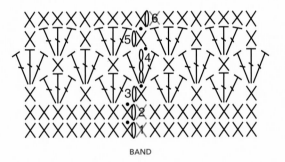

BAND

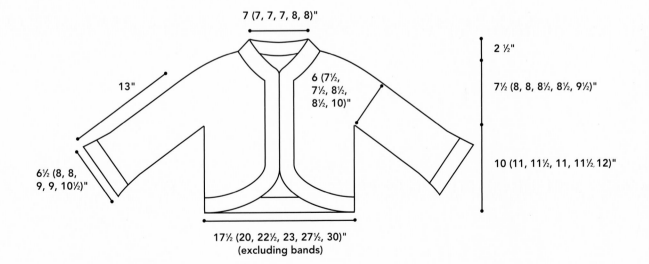

7 (7, 7, 7, 8, 8)"

2 ½"

13"

6 (7½, 7½, 8½, 8½, 10)"

7½ (8, 8, 8½, 8½, 9½)"

6½ (8, 8, 9, 9, 10½)"

10 (11, 11½, 11, 11½, 12)"

17½ (20, 22½, 23, 27½, 30)"
(excluding bands)

MEI-MEI

This tiny jacket is the little sister of the cardigan family. Crocheted in a luxurious cashmere blend, it is the perfect year-round take-along cozy for your neck and shoulders. Think of those situations where you can't control the room temperature—say at a restaurant or the movies, in someone else's car, or traveling—and you'll get the picture. Make it in a fancy novelty yarn to wear not for warmth, but for the compliments! Make the In-Line button link (page 136) and close the front if you like.

MEI-MEI

Skill Level	INTERMEDIATE	

Size

Finished bust: 35 (40, 45, 50, 55, 60)" (88 [101.5, 114, 127, 140, 152.5]cm), not including bands

Materials

Lion Brand Cashmere Blend; 72% merino wool, 14% cashmere, 14% nylon; 1½ oz (40g)/84 yd (77m)

5 (5, 6, 6, 7, 8) balls in #098 Cream

Size J-10 (6mm) crochet hook

Size I-9 (5.5mm) crochet hook for finishing

Gauge

Using J-10 (6 mm) or larger hook, 10 BASE CH/SC or sc = 4" (10cm)

In Shell and V pattern, one repeat (SH, V) = 2½" (6.5cm), 6 rows in pattern = 4" (10cm)

In sc of finishing, 12 sc = 4" (10cm)

Special Stitches

See Cinnabar, page 67

This version is very short and sleeveless, with the same bolero shaping as Mocha Roca (page 76).

YOKE

Make same as Cinnabar (page 66) through Body Row 2.

BODY

Beginning with PATT ROW 1 (2, 1, 2, 1, 2), work even on 14 (16, 18, 20, 22, 24) pattern repeats for 1 (2, 3, 4, 3, 4) more rows, or for desired length of body before bolero shaping. End by working PATT ROW 1.

Adjusting for length

Omit rows here for a shorter jacket, and end by working PATT ROW 1. Add rows here for a longer jacket, and end by working PATT ROW 1.

BOLERO SHAPING

Row 1–4: Same as Mocha Roca Bolero Shaping Rows 1–4 (page 78), turn, continue with finishing below—10 (12, 14, 16, 18, 20) pattern repeats.

FINISHING

Finish entire edge with a RS round of sc, working firmly to gauge 12 sc = 4" (10cm), holding in some of the fullness across lower edge. Switch to smaller hook if necessary to obtain gauge.

Rnd 1 (RS): Ch 1, continue same as Mocha Roca Body Band Rnd 1 (page 79), make sc around, marking both front neck 3-sc corners in same way, ending with sl st in beg sc, turn.

Rnd 2 (WS): Ch 1, *sc in each sc to next corner sc, 3 sc in corner sc*; repeat from * to *, sc in each sc to end, sl st in beg sc, turn.

Rnd 3 (RS): Repeat Rnd 2, fasten off.

ARMHOLES

Finish armholes with one round in pattern.

Rnd 1: Same as Cinnabar Rnd 1 (page 70). Fasten off.

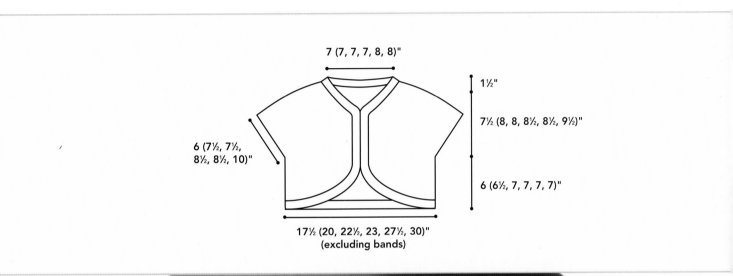

7 (7, 7, 7, 8, 8)"

1½"

7½ (8, 8, 8½, 8½, 9½)"

6 (7½, 7½, 8½, 8½, 10)"

6 (6½, 7, 7, 7, 7)"

17½ (20, 22½, 23, 27½, 30)"
(excluding bands)

|5|
LAYER IT ON
VESTS

my favorite crocheted garments are vests. I like how I can sidestep having to make two sleeves that are exactly the same. And I appreciate how you can use practically any yarn and not too terribly much of it. A good vest can hide many sins. I would love for every crocheter to have a trusty pattern for a vest that can be whipped up whenever the mood strikes and that looks terrific.

YARN NOTES

The pieces in this chapter are designed for mid-weight yarns, from DK to light and medium worsted weight, ball band symbol 4 or sometimes 3, with knitting gauge around 18 to 20 sts per 4" (10cm). Fibers that are lightweight for their thickness will work well, particularly for a longer length or plus size. Blends containing microfiber with wool or cotton are wonderful; they can be crocheted to worsted-weight gauge yet won't weigh you down. Feel free to use any yarn or combination of yarns that work to gauge.

SIZE FINDER

Choose the size that is closest to your bust measurement for a close, body-skimming fit; add 1–2" (2.5–5cm) of ease for a standard fit, or size up even more for a big vest fit. The deep neckline allows for plenty of room at the top for most figures, but if you are particularly full-busted, do the bust short rows. If your hips are more than 3" (7.5cm) larger than your bust and you want to make a longer version that covers your hips, you may wish to size up or look at the longer Eve's Rib Tunic (page 94) option for hip shaping.

GALENA

This lacy pullover vest is designed for layering, with a deeply scooped U-neck, slightly dropped armholes to accommodate the clothes underneath, and small capped shoulders. Make it long to wear belted, even longer for a cute jumper.

GALENA

Skill Level	INTERMEDIATE	

INSTRUCTIONS

Size

Finished bust: 34 (37, 41, 45, 49, 52, 56)" (86 [94, 104, 114, 124.5, 132, 142]cm)

Materials

Lana Grossa Luxor; 51% merino wool, 49% microfiber polyamide; 1¾ oz (50g)/164 yd (150m)

3 (4, 4, 5, 5, 6, 6) balls in #005 (silver)

Size J-10 (6mm) crochet hook

Size I-9 (5.5mm) crochet hook, if needed for finishing to gauge

Gauge

11 BASE CH/SC or 11 sc = 4" (10cm)

In pattern, 2 repeats (shell, sc) and 6 rows = 3¾" (9.5cm)

SCALLOP EDGE

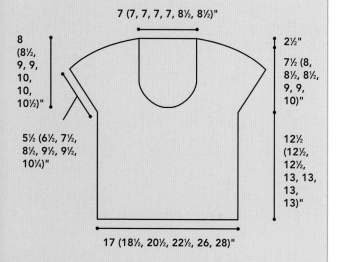

7 (7, 7, 7, 7, 8½, 8½)"

8 (8½, 9, 9, 10, 10, 10½)"

2½"

7½ (8, 8½, 8½, 9, 9, 10)"

5½ (6½, 7½, 8½, 9½, 9½, 10¼)"

12½ (12½, 12½, 13, 13, 13, 13)"

17 (18½, 20½, 22½, 26, 28)"

YOKE

BASE CH/SC 25 (25, 25, 25, 25, 29, 29) to measure 9 (9, 9, 9, 10½, 10½)" (23 [23, 23, 23, 26.5, 26.5]cm) stretched. Set up 6 (6, 6, 6, 6, 7, 7) pattern repeats as follows.

Row 1: Ch 1, sc in first sc, [sk next sc, SH in next sc, sk next sc, sc in next sc] 6 (6, 6, 6, 6, 7, 7) times, end with sc in last sc, turn—6 (6, 6, 6, 6, 7, 7) shells.

Row 2 (inc): Ch 5, [(dc, ch 2) 3 times, dc] in first sc for inc corner, sc in second dc of next sh, INC-SH in next sc for corner, sc in second dc of next sh, [SH in next sc, sc in second dc of next sh] 3 (3, 3, 3, 3, 4, 4) times, INC-SH in next sc, sc in second dc of next sh, INC-SH in last sc, turn—7 (7, 7, 7, 7, 8, 8) pattern repeats.

Mark the middle dc at each corner, and move markers up as you go.

Row 3 (inc): Ch 5, dc in first dc, *over inc-sh work (sc in second dc, INC-SH in third dc, sc in fourth dc), SH in next sc*; repeat from * to *, [sc in second dc of next sh, SH in next sc] to next inc-sh, repeat from * to *,except omit last SH, instead end with (dc, ch 2, dc) in third ch of tch, turn—10 (10, 10, 10, 10, 11, 11) pattern repeats.

Front neck edges now worked even for depth of U-neck as follows:

Size 34

Row 4–11: YOKE 4, PATT ROW 2, YOKE 1–2, PATT ROW 1, YOKE 3–4, PATT ROW 2—23 pattern repeats.

Size 37

Row 4–12: YOKE 5, YOKE 2, PATT ROW 1, YOKE 3–4, PATT ROW 2, YOKE 1–2, PATT ROW 1—27 pattern repeats.

Special Stitches

SH: (Dc, ch 2, dc, ch 2, dc) in same st or sp.

INC-SH: [Dc, (ch 2, dc) 4 times] in same st or sp.

SCALLOP: (Sl st, ch 2, hdc) in same st or sp.

Stitch Pattern

STITCH PATTERN (IN ROWS)

PATT ROW 1: Ch 1, sc in first dc, [SH in next sc, sc in second dc of next sh] to end, placing last sc in third ch of tch, turn.

PATT ROW 2: Ch 5, dc in first sc, [sc in second dc of next sh, SH in next sc] to end, except omit last SH, instead end with (dc, ch 2, dc) in last sc, turn.

BASIC SHELL PATTERN IN ROWS

YOKE STITCH PATTERN (IN ROWS)

YOKE 1 (as PATT ROW 1) (inc): Ch 1, sc in first dc, *work in pattern to next corner sc, INC-SH in corner sc, sc in second dc of next sh*; repeat from * to * 3 times, work in pattern to end, ending with sc in third ch of tch, turn.

YOKE 2 (as PATT ROW 2) (even over inc): Ch 5, dc in first sc, *work in pattern to next inc-sh, over inc-sh work (sc in second dc, SH in third dc, sc in 4th dc), SH in next sc*; repeat from * to * 3 times, work in pattern to end, ending with (dc, ch 2, dc) in last sc, turn.

YOKE 3 (as PATT ROW 2) (inc): Ch 5, dc in first sc, *work in pat-

tern to next corner sc, INC-SH in corner sc*; repeat from * to * 3 times, work in pattern to end, ending with (dc, ch 2, dc) in last sc, turn.

YOKE 4 (as PATT ROW 1) (even over inc): Ch 1, sc in first dc, *work in pattern to next inc-sh, over inc-sh work (sc in second dc, SH in third dc, sc in 4th dc)*; repeat from * to * 3 times, work in pattern to end, ending with sc in third ch of tch, turn.

YOKE 5 (as PATT ROW 1) (onc over inc): Ch 1, sc in first dc, *work in pattern to next inc-sh, over inc-sh work (sc in second dc, INC-SH in third dc, sc in 4th dc); repeat from * to * 3 times, work in pattern to end, ending with sc in third ch of tch, turn.

YOKE 6 (as PATT ROW 2) (inc over inc): Ch 5, dc in first sc, *work in pattern to next inc-sh, over inc-sh work (sc in second dc, INC-SH in third dc, sc in 4th dc); repeat from * to * 3 times, work in pattern to end, ending with (dc, ch 2, dc) in last sc, turn.

STITCH PATTERN (IN ROUNDS)

PATT RND 1: Ch 1, sc in same dc, [SH in next sc, sc in second dc of next sh] around, except omit last sc, instead end with sl st in beg sc, turn.

PATT RND 2: Ch 5, dc in same sc, [sc in second dc of next sh, SH in next sc] around, except omit last SH, instead end with dc in same sc as beg, ch 2, sl st in third ch of beg ch, turn.

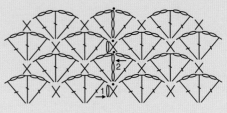

BASIC SHELL PATTERN IN RNDS

Sizes 41 (45)

Row 4–13: YOKE 5–6, YOKE 4, PATT ROW 2, YOKE 1–2, PATT ROW 1, YOKE 3–4, PATT ROW 2—31 pattern repeats.

Sizes 49 (52)

Row 4–14: YOKE 5–6, YOKE 5, YOKE 2, PATT ROW 1, YOKE 3–4, PATT ROW 2, YOKE 1–2, PATT ROW 1—35 (36) pattern repeats.

Size 56

Row 4–15: YOKE 5–6 for 2 times, YOKE 4, PATT ROW 2, YOKE 1–2, PATT ROW 1, YOKE 3–4, PATT ROW 2—40 pattern repeats.

UNDERARM JOINING

23 (27, 31, 31, 35, 36, 40) pattern repeats, with a sc at

each marked corner. Join front and back with additional sts at underarms.

Sizes 34 (41, 45, 56)

Join Row: Ch 1, sc in first dc, *work in pattern to next corner sc, SH in corner sc, ch 1, BASE CH/SC 5 (5, 9, 9) for underarm, sk 5 (7, 7, 9) repeats of armhole, SH in next corner sc*; repeat from * to *, work in pattern to end, placing sc in third ch of tch, turn.

Sizes 37 (49, 52)

Join Row: Ch 5, dc in first sc, *work in pattern to next corner sc, SH in corner sc, ch 1, BASE CH/SC 5 (9, 9) for underarm, sk 6 (8, 8) repeats of armhole, SH in next corner sc*; repeat from * to *, work in pattern to end, ending with (dc, ch 2, dc) in last sc, turn.

Stop here for Insight, continued on page 100, and 4-S Vest, page 106.

BODY

Fill in pattern over underarms and join front neck with additional stitches as follows.

Sizes 34 (41)

Rnd 1: Ch 5, dc in first sc, *work in pattern to underarm base ch/sc, sk next 2 sc, SH in next sc, sk rem 2 sc, sc in second dc of next sh*; repeat from * to *, work in pattern to end, ending with (dc, ch 2, dc) in last sc, ch 1, BASE CH/SC 11 for front neck, sl st in third ch of beg ch, fasten off.

Size 37

Rnd 1: Ch 1, sc in first dc, work SIZE 34 RND 1 from * to * twice, work in pattern to end, placing last sc in third ch of tch, ch 1, BASE CH/SC 11 for front neck, sl st in beg sc, fasten off.

Sizes 45 (56)

Rnd 1: Ch 5, dc in first sc, *work in pattern to underarm base ch/sc, sk next sc of underarm, SH in next sc, sk next 2 sc, sc in next sc, sk next 2 sc, SH in next sc, sk rem sc, sc in second dc of next sh*; repeat from * to *, work in pattern to end, ending with (dc, ch 1, dc) in last sc, ch 1, BASE CH/SC 11 (15) for front neck, sl st in third ch of beg ch, fasten off.

Sizes 49 (52)

Rnd 1: Ch 1, sc in first dc, work SIZE 45 RND 1 from * to * twice, work in pattern to end, placing last sc in third ch of tch, ch 1, BASE CH/SC 11 (15) for front neck, sl st in beg sc, fasten off.

All Sizes

Turn, move join to center of next underarm, which is the second dc of shell for SIZES 34, (37, 41) and a sc for SIZES 45 (49, 52, 56). Work now toward the back, fill in pattern over front neck.

Sizes 34 (41)

Rnd 2: Join with sl st in dc at center of underarm, ch 1, sc in same dc, work in pattern, placing sc in second dc of sh before neck base ch/sc, [sk next sc, SH in next sc, sk next sc, sc in next sc] twice, sk next sc, SH in next sc, sk rem sc, work in pattern to end, ending with sl st in beg sc, turn—18 (22) pattern repeats.

Size 37

Rnd 2: Join with sl st in dc at center of underarm, ch 1, sc in same dc, work in pattern, placing SH in last sc before neck base ch/sc, [sk next sc, sc in next sc, sk next sc, SH in next sc] twice, sk next sc, sc in next sc, sk rem sc of base ch/sc, work in pattern to end, ending with sl st in beg sc, turn—20 pattern repeats.

Size 45

Rnd 2: Join with sl st in sc at center of underarm, ch 5, dc in same sc, work in pattern, placing sc in second dc of sh before neck base ch/sc, [sk next sc, SH in next sc, sk next sc, sc in next sc] twice, sk next sc, SH in next sc, sk rem sc, work in pattern to end, ending with dc in same sc as beg, ch 2, sl st in third ch of beg ch, turn—24 pattern repeats.

Size 49

Rnd 2: Join with sl st in sc at center of underarm, ch 5, dc in same sc, work in pattern, placing SH in last sc before neck base ch/sc, [sk next sc, sc in next sc, sk next sc, SH in next sc] twice, sk next sc, sc in next sc, sk rem sc of base ch/sc, work in pattern to end, ending with dc in same sc as beg, ch 2, sl st in third ch of beg ch, turn—26 pattern repeats.

Size 52

Rnd 2: Join with sl st in sc at center of underarm, ch 5, dc in same sc, work in pattern, placing SH in last sc before neck base ch/sc, [sk next sc, sc in next sc, sk next sc, SH in next sc] 3 times, sk next sc, sc in next sc, sk rem base ch/sc, work in pattern to end, ending with dc in same sc as beg, ch 2, sl st in third ch of beg ch, turn—28 pattern repeats.

Size 56

Rnd 2: Join with sl st in sc at center of underarm, ch 5, dc in same sc, work in pattern, placing sc in second dc of sh before neck base ch/sc, [sk next sc, SH in next sc, sk next sc, sc in next sc] 3 times, sk next sc, SH in next sc, sk rem base ch/sc, work in pattern to end, ending with dc in same sc as beg, ch 2, sl st in third ch of beg ch, turn—30 pattern repeats.

Adjusting for full bust

Turn, now moving toward the front. All sizes are at the center stitch at underarm; for SIZES 34 (37, 41) that is a sc, for SIZES 45 (49, 52, 56) that is a dc. Put the loop on the hook on hold. SIZES 34 (37, 41), join new yarn with sl st in second dc of next shell. SIZES 45 (49, 52, 56), sk rem sts of same sh, sk next sc, join with sl st in second dc of next shell.

Short Row A: [SH in next sc, sc in second dc of next shell] 8 (9, 10, 10, 11, 12, 13) times across front, except omit last sc, instead end with sl st in second dc of sh, turn.

Short Row B: Sl st in next dc, each of next 2 ch and next dc, [SH in next sc, sc in second dc of next sh] 7 (8, 9, 9, 10, 11, 12) times, except omit last sc, instead end with sl st in second dc of sh, fasten off. Put loop on hold back on hook.

Stop here for Eve's Rib Tunic, continued on page 96.

BODY CONTINUED

Note: If you made bust short rows, ignore the sl sts and work the next round in pattern as facing into the dc containing the sl st turns.

Work even on 18 (20, 22, 24, 26, 28, 30) pattern repeats for 17 (17, 17, 18, 18, 18, 18) rounds, ending with PATT RND 1.

Adjusting for length

Vest shown is high hip length, approximately 5" (12.5cm) down from waist. For Petite or shorter vest, omit 2 pattern rounds (1½" [3.8cm]) or more as desired. For Tall or longer vest, add 2 pattern rounds (1½" [3.8cm]) or more as desired.

FINISHING

LOWER EDGING

There is no obvious RS or WS until you make that designation here. All sizes turn, RS now facing, make scal-

lop edging around bottom as follows.

Scallop Rnd (RS): *[sl st, ch 2, hdc] for SCALLOP in next ch-sp, SCALLOP in next sc, SCALLOP in next ch-sp*; repeat from * to * 17 (19, 21, 23, 25, 27, 29) times, sl st in same ch-sp as beg, fasten off.

NECK EDGE

With RS facing, join yarn with sl st in 13th (13th, 13th, 13th, 13th, 15th, 15th) base ch at center back of neck, make one round sc working firmly to gauge of 11 sc = 4" (10cm). If needed, switch to a smaller hook to achieve tighter gauge.

Sc Rnd (RS): Ch 1, sc in same ch, sc in each of rem 12 (12, 12, 12, 12, 14, 14) ch of back neck, sc in next sc row edge of front neck, 2 sc in next dc row edge, [2 sc in next dc row edge, sc in next sc row edge] 5 (5, 6, 6, 6, 6, 7) times, 2 sc in next dc row edge, sc in each of next 11 (11, 11, 11, 11, 15, 15) ch of front neck, repeat between [ ] 5 (5, 6, 6, 6, 6, 7) times, 2 sc in each of next 2 dc row edges, sc in next sc row edge, sc in each of next 12 (12, 12, 12, 12, 14, 14) ch of back neck, sl st in beg sc—76 (76, 82, 82, 82, 90, 96) sc.

Do not turn. With RS still facing, make scallop edging as follows.

Scallop Rnd (RS): Ch 2, hdc in same sc [sk next 2 sc, SCALLOP in next sc] around, sk rem 2 sc, sl st in same sc as beg, fasten off.

ARMHOLE EDGE

With RS facing, join yarn with sl st in 3rd (3rd, 3rd, 5th, 5th, 5th, 5th) base ch at center of underarm.

Scallop Rnd (RS): Ch 2, hdc in same ch, [sk next ch, SCALLOP in next ch] 1 (1, 1, 2, 2, 2, 2) times, SCALLOP in next dc row edge, [SCALLOP in each of next 2 ch-sp, SCALLOP in next sc] 4 (5, 6, 7, 8, 8, 9) times, SCALLOP in each of next 2 ch-sp of last sh, SCALLOP in next dc row edge, [SCALLOP in next ch of underarm, sk next ch] 1 (1, 1, 2, 2, 2, 2) times, sl st in same ch as beg, fasten off.

Make Armhole Edge around second armhole in same way.

EVE'S RIB TUNIC

This version of a U-neck vest offers more hip cover-age and ease thanks to sets of pattern increases that start just below the waist. If your figure can carry the added volume, make the optional collar, an exagger-ated cowl in soft ribbing, and the ribbed armbands.

EVE'S RIB TUNIC

Skill Level | INTERMEDIATE | ④ MEDIUM

Size

Finished bust: 34 (37, 41, 45, 49, 52, 56)" (86 [94, 104, 114, 124.5, 132, 142]cm)

Materials

Caron Simply Soft Shadows; Art.SHA100; 100% acrylic; 3 oz (85g)/153 yd (140m)

5 (5, 6, 6, 7, 7, 8) skeins in #0005 Soft Merino

Size J-10 (6mm) crochet hook

Size I-9 (5.5mm) crochet hook, if needed for finishing to gauge

Gauge

11 BASE CH/SC or 11 sc = 4" (10cm)

2 repeats (shell, sc) and 6 rows = 3¾" (9.5cm)

With hook needed, in sctbl rib, 12 st and 12 rows = 4" (10cm) as crocheted

When worn, stitch gauge will compress and row gauge will stretch, as is the nature of ribbing.

Special Stitches

See Galena, page 91

Sctbl: make sc by inserting hook through back loop only of next st.

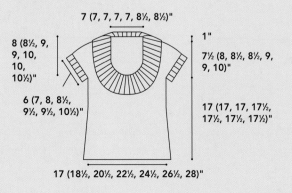

7 (7, 7, 7, 7, 8½, 8½)"

8 (8½, 9, 9, 10, 10, 10½)"

1"

7½ (8, 8½, 8½, 9, 9, 10)"

6 (7, 8, 8½, 9½, 9½, 10½)"

17 (17, 17, 17½, 17½, 17½, 17½)"

17 (18½, 20½, 22½, 24½, 26½, 28)"

INSTRUCTIONS

YOKE

Make in the same way as Galena (page 90) through Body RND 2, making bust short rows if desired.

BODY

Work even on 18 (20, 22, 24, 26, 28, 30) pattern repeats for 8 (9, 9, 9, 10, 10, 9) more rounds, ending with PATT RND 1 (2, 2, 1, 2, 2, 1).

HIP SHAPING

Sizes 34 (45, 56)

Rnd 1: Ch 5, dc in same sc, sc in second dc of next sh, *[SH in next sc, sc in second dc of next sh] 2 (3, 4) times, INC-SH in next sc, sc in second dc of next sh, repeat between [ ] 2 (3, 4) times, INC-SH in next sc, sc in second dc of next sh, repeat between [ ] 3 (4, 5) times*; repeat from * to *, except omit last SH, instead end with dc in same sc as beg, ch 2, sl st in third ch of beg ch, turn.

Rnd 2: Ch 1, sc in same dc, *work in pattern to next inc-sh, over inc-sh work (sc in second dc, SH in third dc, sc in fourth dc)*; repeat from * to * 3 times, work in pattern to end, ending with sl st in beg sc, turn—22 (28, 34) pattern repeats.

Rnd 3–16: Work even in pattern for 14 rounds, ending with PATT RND 1.

Sizes 37 (41, 49, 52)

Rnd 1: Ch 1, sc in same dc, *[SH in next sc, sc in second

dc of next sh] 3 (3, 4, 4) times, INC-SH in next sc, sc in second dc of next sh, repeat between [ ] 2 (3, 3, 4) times, INC-SH in next sc, sc in second dc of next sh, repeat between [ ] 3 (3, 4, 4) times*; repeat from * to *, except omit last sc, instead end with sl st in beg sc, turn.

Rnd 2: Ch 5, dc in same sc, *work in pattern to next inc-sh, over inc-sh work (sc in second dc, SH in third dc, sc in fourth dc)*; repeat from * to * 3 times, work in pattern to end, ending with dc in same sc as beg, ch 2, sl st in third ch of beg ch, turn—24 (26, 30, 32) pattern repeats.

Rnd 3–15: Work even in pattern for 13 rounds, ending with PATT RND 1.

Adjusting for length

Length is approximately 11" (28cm) from waist. Omit or add rows as desired. End by working PATT RND 1.

FINISHING

You may finish Eve's Rib Tunic same way as Galena (page 93), finishing with scallop edging at lower edge, neckline, and armholes. I prefer the lower edge of this tunic left as is, with no added bulk. Fasten off after last round.

COLLAR (OPTIONAL)

Sctbl ribbing compresses itself without any change in yarn tension, so you may find you can work the collar at a gauge of 12 sc and 12 rows = 4" (10cm) without changing hook size. But if needed, switch to a smaller hook. Increase the fullness of the ribbing by adding an extra row every third row as follows.

Note: Be particularly vigilant in working the first and last sc of each row; they can be difficult to see. Check your work and count stitches often.

SC Rnd (RS): Same as Galena SC Rnd (page 93), do not turn—76 (76, 82, 82, 82, 90, 96) sc.

Row 1 (RS): Ch 1, insert hook in same sc, BASE CH/SC 15, turn.

Row 2 (WS): Ch 1, sctbl in each of next 15 sc, sl st in next sc of neck, turn.

Row 3 (RS) (short row): Sk sl st, sctbl in each of next 15 sc, turn.

Row 4 (WS): Ch 1, sctbl in each of next 15 sc, sl st in each of next 2 sc of neck, turn.

Row 5 (RS): Sk 2 sl st, sctbl in each of next 15 sc, turn. Repeat Rows 2–5 around sc of neck edge, end by working Row 5 (5, 5, 5, 5, 4, 4), fasten off, leaving long tail for seaming.

Thread tail on yarn needle (I like a ball end for this task). Holding last row together with beginning base ch/sc, matching sts, whip stitch 15 sts together, going through 2 strands of base ch edge and through back loop only of sc edge each time. Fasten off.

ARMBANDS (OPTIONAL)

These bands are meant to be the same circumference as armholes, neither too loose nor too tight. Work to the same ribbing gauge as the collar, switching to the smaller hook if needed.

Sc Rnd (RS): With RS facing, join yarn with sl st in 3rd (3rd, 3rd, 5th, 5th, 5th, 5th) base ch at center of underarm, ch 1, sc in same ch, sc in remaining 2 (2, 2, 3, 3, 3, 3) ch, 2 sc in next dc row edge, [sc in each dc and ch-sp of next sh, sc in next sc] 5 (6, 7, 7, 8, 8, 9) times, except omit last sc, 2 sc in next dc row edge, sc in remaining 2 (2, 2, 3, 3, 3, 3) ch of underarm, sl st in beg sc—38 (44, 50, 54, 60, 60, 66) sc.

Row 1 (RS): Do not turn, ch 1, insert hook in same sc, BASE CH/SC 4, turn.

Row 2 (WS): Ch 1, sctbl in each of next 4 sc, sl st in each of next 2 sc of armhole edge, turn.

Row 3 (RS): Sk 2 sl st, sctbl in each of next 4 sc, turn. Repeat Rows 2–3 around, end by working Row 2, with sl st in last sc, fasten off, leaving a few inches of tail for seaming.

Seam 4 sts of armband in the same way as the collar. Make band on second armhole in the same way.

INSIGHT

This version features an open front with a more exaggerated plunging neckline and string ties below the fullest part of the bust, making it so pretty and curvaceous.

Size Finder: For the look of a nipped-in waist, size down for a slimmer fit. Or choose to size up, as shown here, for a loose, breezy vest.

Yarn Note: The microfiber in this yarn makes it deliciously soft and an astonishingly lightweight cotton blend for its gauge, as you can tell from the yardage per ball. This is a godsend when making a longer garment in a larger size.

Skill Level	INTERMEDIATE	4 MEDIUM

INSIGHT

INSTRUCTIONS

This vest uses the same U-Neck construction as Galena (page 88), but is left open in front.

Size
Finished bust: 34 (37, 41, 45, 49, 52, 56)" (86 [94, 104, 114, 124.5, 132, 142]cm)

Materials
Lana Grossa New Cotton; 60% cotton, 40% microfiber polyamide; 1¾ oz (50g)/153 yd (140m)

5 (5, 6, 7, 8, 8, 9) balls in #9 violet

Size J-10 (6mm) crochet hook

Size I-9 (5.5mm) crochet hook, if needed for finishing to gauge

Special Stitches
See Galena, page 91

YOKE

Make same as Galena (page 90) through JOIN ROW. Continuing to work back and forth, fill in pattern at underarms as follows.

Sizes 34 (41)
Row 1: Ch 5, dc in first sc, *work in pattern, placing sc in second dc of sh before base ch/sc of underarm, sk next 2 sc of underarm, SH in next sc, sk remaining 2 sc*; repeat from * to *, work in pattern to end, ending with (dc, ch 2, dc) in last sc, turn—15 (19) pattern repeats.

Size 37
Row 1: Ch 1, sc in first dc, work Size 34 Row 1 from * to * twice, work in pattern to end, ending with sc in third ch of tch, turn—17 pattern repeats.

Sizes 45 (56)
Row 1: Ch 5, dc in first sc, *work in pattern, placing sc in second dc of sh before base ch/sc of underarm, sk next sc of underarm, SH in next sc, sk next 2 sc, sc in next sc, sk next 2 sc, SH in next sc, sk remaining sc*; repeat from * to *, work in pattern to end, ending with (dc, ch 2, dc) in last sc, turn—21 (26) pattern repeats.

Sizes 49 (52)

Row 1: Ch 1, sc in first dc, work SIZE 45 ROW 1 from * to * twice, work in pattern to end, ending with sc in third ch of tch, turn—23 (24) pattern repeats.

All Sizes

15 (17, 19, 21, 23, 24, 26) pattern repeats

Sizes 34 (41, 45, 56)

Row 2–3: PATT ROWS 1–2.

Sizes 37 (49, 52)

Row 2: PATT ROW 2.

Adjusting for full bust

Matching short rows are worked on each side of fronts. For SIZES 34 (41, 49, 52), there is a sh at center of each underarm; for SIZES 37 (45, 56), there is a sc at center of each underarm.

First Side Short Rows

Begin as PATT ROW 1, work in pattern for 2 (3, 3, 4, 4, 4, 5) shells, sl st in second dc of next sh, turn. Sl st in first dc, in each of next 2 ch and next dc, SH in next sc, work in pattern to end, end as PATT ROW 2. Put the loop on the hook on hold.

Second Side Short Rows

Turn, sk to other underarm. SIZES 34 (41, 49, 52): sk sh at center of underarm and next sc. SIZES 37 (45, 56): sk sc at center of underarm.

Join new yarn with sl st in second dc of next sh, SH in next sc, work in pattern to end, end as PATT ROW 1, turn. Begin as PATT ROW 2, work in pattern to last sh of short row, sl st in second dc of last sh, fasten off. Pick up loop on hold, and continue with next row.

Note: If you made bust short rows, ignore the sl sts and work the next round in pattern as facing into the dc containing the sl st turns.

All Sizes

Next Row: Work PATT ROW 1 even on 15 (17, 19, 21, 23, 24, 25) pattern repeats, fasten off.

Stop here for Outta Sight, continued on page 124. Stop here for Outta Sight, continued on page 124.

BODY

Turn, add sts at each end of next row for front neck as follows.

Row 1: BASE CH/SC 6 (6, 6, 6, 6, 8, 8) for front neck, SH in first sc of last row, work in pattern, placing SH in last sc, ch 1, BASE CH/SC 6 (6, 6, 6, 6, 8, 8), turn.

Sizes 34 (37, 41, 45, 49)

Row 2: Ch 5, dc in first sc of base ch/sc, sk next sc, sc in next sc, sk next sc, SH in next sc, sk remaining base ch/sc, work in pattern, placing sc in second dc of sh before base ch/sc, sk next sc, SH in next sc, sk next sc, sc in next sc, sk next sc, (dc, ch 2, dc) in last sc, turn.

Sizes 52 (56)

Row 2: Ch 1, sc in first base ch/sc, sk next sc, SH in next sc, sk next sc, sc in next sc, sk next sc, SH in next sc, sk remaining base ch/sc, work in pattern, placing sc in second dc of sh before base ch/sc, sk next sc, SH in next sc, sk next sc, sc in next sc, sk next sc, SH in next sc, sk next sc, sc in last sc, turn.

All Sizes

Work even on 18 (20, 22, 24, 26, 28, 30) pattern repeats for 6 (6, 5, 5, 5, 5, 5) rows to waist-length, end by working PATT ROW 2 (2, 1, 1, 1, 2, 2).

Stop here for 4-S Vest, continued on page 106. Stop here for 4-S Vest, continued on page 106.

SKIRT

Make 2 increases, one to each side of center back as follows.

Sizes 34 (37, 52, 56)

Row 1: Ch 1, sc in first dc, [SH in next sc, sc in second dc of next sh] 7 (8, 11, 12) times, INC-SH in next sc, sc in second dc of next sh, repeat between [ ] 2 (2, 4, 4) times, INC-SH in next dc, sc in second dc of next sh, repeat between [ ] 7 (8, 11, 12) times to end, placing last sc in third ch of tch, turn.

Sizes 41 (45, 49)

Row 1: Ch 5, dc in first sc, sc in second dc of next sh, [SH in next sc, sc in second dc of next sh] 8 (9, 10) times, INC-SH in next sc, sc in second dc of next sh, repeat between [ ] 3 times, INC-SH in next sc, sc in second dc of next sh, repeat between [ ] 8 (9, 10) times, ending with (dc, ch 2, dc) in last sc, turn.

Sizes 34 (37, 52, 56)

Row 2: Ch 5, dc in first sc, *work in pattern to next inc-sh, over inc-sh work (sc in second dc, SH in third dc, sc in fourth dc), SH in next sc*; repeat from * to *, work in pattern to end, ending with (dc, ch 2, dc) in last sc, turn.

Sizes 41 (45, 49)

Row 2: Ch 1, sc in first dc, *work in pattern to next inc-sh, over inc-sh work (sc in second dc, SH in third dc, sc in fourth dc), SH in next sc*; repeat from * to *, work in pattern to end, ending with sc in third ch of tch, turn.

All Sizes

Work even on 20 (22, 24, 26, 28, 30, 32) pattern repeats for 15 (15, 16, 16, 16, 17, 17) more rows, end by working PATT ROW 1.

Adjusting for length

Add or omit rows in pattern until desired length, end by working PATT ROW 1.

FINISHING

Finishing is crocheted firmly to gauge of 11 sc = 4" (10cm). Switch to smaller hook if needed to obtain gauge. There is no obvious RS or WS until you make that determination now. Do not turn, RS now facing, rotate and work sc around front and neck edges as follows.

Sc Rnd (RS): Ch 1, [2 sc in each dc row edge, sc in each sc row edge] to front U-neck base ch, 3 sc in first base ch for corner, sc in remaining ch of front neck, repeat between [ ] to back neck base ch, sc in each base ch of back neck, repeat between [ ] to other front neck base ch, sc in each base ch, with 3 sc in last base ch for corner, repeat between [ ] to bottom, ending with 2 sc in last dc row edge, sl st in first sc of bottom edge. NOTE: Exact number is not critical, but try to have the same number at each side of front. Make scallop edge and string ties at once as follows.

Scallop Rnd (RS): Working across shells of bottom edge, ch 2, hdc in same sc, [(sl st, ch 2, hdc—SCALLOP) in each of next 2 ch-2 sps, SCALLOP in next sc] across, ending with SCALLOP in last sc of bottom edge, rotate and work across sc of front edge, *[sk next 2 sc, SCALLOP in next sc] to U-neck corner. Compensate for stitch count by adjusting the number of sc skipped (1 or 2) so you end up with a sl st in second sc of 3-sc corner, (ch 50, sl st in second ch from hook, sl st in remaining 48 ch, sl st in same corner sc) for tie, ch 2, hdc in same sc*; repeat from * to *, again adjusting stitch count at corner to mirror placement of other corner and tie, make scallops same as before to end of front, sl st in same sc as beg of round, fasten off.

ARMHOLES

Finish armholes with scallop edging in the same way as Galena (page 93).

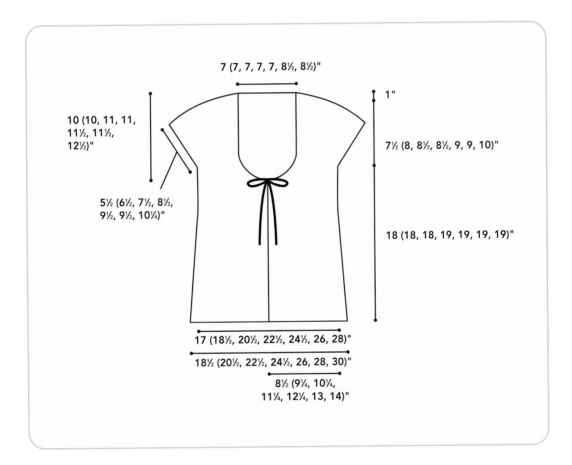

7 (7, 7, 7, 7, 8½, 8½)"

1"

10 (10, 11, 11, 11½, 11½, 12½)"

7½ (8, 8½, 8½, 9, 9, 10)"

5½ (6½, 7½, 8½, 9½, 9½, 10¼)"

18 (18, 18, 19, 19, 19, 19)"

17 (18½, 20½, 22½, 24½, 26, 28)"

18½ (20½, 22½, 24½, 26, 28, 30)"

8½ (9¼, 10¼, 11¼, 12¼, 13, 14)"

4-S VEST

Short, *striped*, *sassy*, *shell* vest, that is. This version is quick to make, in three colors, cropped to waist-length, with a three-button front.

Yarn Note: If yarn has a personality, then this one is the rugged, outdoorsy type. It is a traditional, lovely firm wool with a sterling organic pedigree, a tad thicker than the other yarns in the book. Crocheted to the same gauge, it produces a firmer fabric that holds its shape, just what you want for a waistcoat. O-Wool is offered in a palette of 13 color-saturated, adult shades; three are featured here.

Size Finder: This version is meant to be short and snug and does not allow for bust short rows or length adjustments. To fit this way, choose the size closest to your bust measurement with little or no ease. Size it down for a tight waistcoat look over a fitted shirt or blouse; size up for a boxy, casual vest to layer over your turtlenecks and sweaters.

4-S VEST

INSTRUCTIONS

Size

Finished bust: 34 (37, 41, 45, 49, 52, 56)" (86 [94, 104, 114, 124.5, 132, 142]cm)

Materials

Vermont Organic Fiber Company O-Wool; 100% certified organic merino wool; 3½ oz (100g)/198 yd (181m)

1 (1, 2, 2, 2, 2, 2) hanks in #5201 Mulberry (A)

1 (1, 1, 1, 2, 2, 2) hanks in #4302 Willow (B)

1 (1, 1, 1, 2, 2, 2) hanks in #2301 Cornflower (C)

3 buttons, ¾" (20mm) diameter

Matching thread and sewing needle

Size J-10 (6mm) crochet hook

Size I-9 (5.5 mm) crochet hook, if needed for finishing to gauge

Gauge

11 BASE CH/SC or 11 sc = 4" (10cm)

In pattern, 2 repeats (shell, sc) and 6 rows = 3¾" (9.5cm)

Special Stitches

See Galena, page 91

Note: To change colors at end of row: Work last st until 2 loops remain on hook, drop old color, YO with new color and complete last st, wrap old yarn once from front to back around new yarn, turn, continue with new yarn. Carry one unused strand loosely up each side, wrapping yarns at each end.

YOKE

Make same as Insight (page 100) to completion of Body, stopping before Skirt, in striping sequence one row of each (A, B, C) throughout as follows.

Make BASE CH/SC and first row in B (B, C, C, A, C, A), then alternate one row of each color in sequence through 24 (24, 25, 25, 25, 25, 27) rows.

Last row worked as PATT ROW 2 in A (PATT ROW 2 in A, PATT ROW 1 in C, PATT ROW 1 in C, PATT ROW 1 in A, PATT ROW 2 in C, PATT ROW 2 in C).

BODY CONTINUED

Work for 5 (5, 6, 6, 8, 9, 9) more rows in pattern and color sequence as established, end by working PATT ROW 1 in C. Fasten off all yarns.

FINISHING

Switch to smaller hook if needed to work to gauge of 11 sc = 4" (10cm).

FRONT EDGES

Sc Rnd (RS): Do not turn, RS now facing, rotate, join A in first sc row edge, ch 1, make SC RND in the same way as Insight (page 102).

Scallop Rnd (RS): Continue with A, making scallop edging in the same way as Insight except omit (ch-50, sl st back) string ties at front neck corners.

ARMHOLES

With A, finish armholes with scallop edging in the same way as Galena (page 93).

BUTTONS

Use the ch-2 lps of scallop edging for buttonholes; choose three scallops most evenly spaced at right front. With needle and thread, sew buttons to sc edging of left front opposite chosen buttonholes, sewing securely through thickness of sc edging.

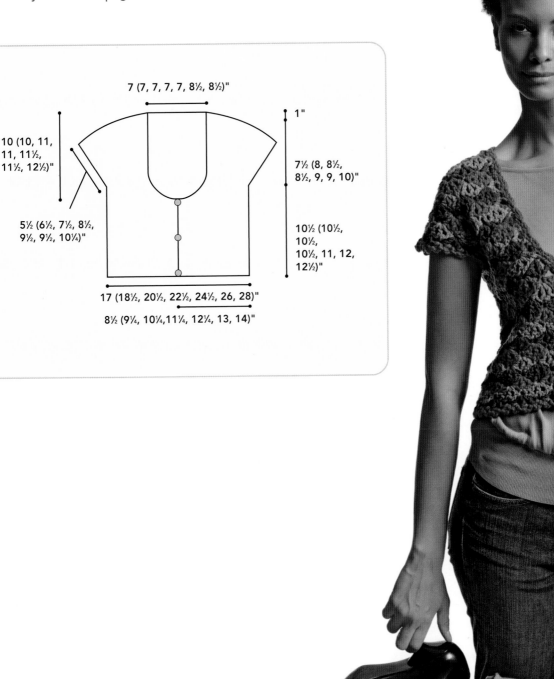

7 (7, 7, 7, 7, 8½, 8½)"

1"

10 (10, 11, 11, 11½, 11½, 12½)"

7½ (8, 8½, 8½, 9, 9, 10)"

5½ (6½, 7½, 8½, 9½, 9½, 10¼)"

10½ (10½, 10½, 10½, 11, 12, 12½)"

17 (18½, 20½, 22½, 24½, 26, 28)"

8½ (9¼, 10¼, 11¼, 12¼, 13, 14)"

|6|
WARM WAYS
COATS

et's not kid ourselves. A crocheted coat is not adequate outerwear in truly foul or frigid conditions, especially if it's any
kind of windy. But when you're feeling chilly, there's nothing
like enveloping yourself in something soft and comforting; it's doubly
nice if that something is decorative as well. The following coats are
adaptations of the tops and vests in the previous chapters, suitable
for layering over your other clothes.

YARN NOTES

See the suggestions listed for each coat style. In general, warmth without excess bulk should be your guideline in choosing yarns for coats that you will use as outerwear. Wool, mohair, alpaca, and multifiber blends, as well as new hollow-core fibers that trap and hold body heat, all make cozy coats. I have used mid- to heavy worsted weight yarns here, but feel free to go even bulkier if you don't mind the weight. Just bear in mind that crocheting a thicker yarn to the stated gauge will make a denser fabric with a firmer drape and might result in a larger garment when finished. If you're looking for a strictly decorative layer, as opposed to true cold-climate outerwear, these coats can go many directions. Use multiple strands of finer yarns, throw in some flash, metallic bling, or luxury novelty yarn for a dressier evening cover-up. Take any of the coats to sweeping ankle length for added drama.

SIZE FINDER

See the suggestions listed for each coat style. In general, the bulkier the yarn, the more ease you will want in the fit.

HARU

Here is a short, slim coat celebrating the variable and idiosyncratic effects you get with long-repeat colorways. It is built on the same pattern as the Tall Latte V-neck pullover (page 50) with a few modifications: left open at the front, made with short sleeves and side vents, to be wrapped and tied with a purchased or crocheted belt or closed with a clasp, button link, or frog. The same open-front construction is also used, in an exploded gauge, for Shannon (page 118).

Yarn Notes: Long have I admired those fabulous yarns with long color repeats, but hesitant was I to incorporate any in my designs. I am so stuck on even, regular color changes and stripes. Hey, I got over it. In an easy-care cotton or blend this would make a handy swim cover-up; with longer sleeves in a dressy yarn, an elegant evening jacket.
Size Finder: This design is meant to be slim-fitting. It offers no fitting options. Choose the size closest to but not larger than your bust or hip measurement, whichever is larger.

HARU

Skill Level | **INTERMEDIATE** | 3 LIGHT

INSTRUCTIONS

Size

Finished bust: 33 (36, 39, 42, 45, 48, 51, 54)" (84 [91, 99, 106.5, 114, 122, 129.5, 137]cm)

Materials

Noro Silk Garden Lite; 45% silk, 45% kid mohair, 10% lamb's wool; 1½ oz (50g)/135 yd (125m)

6 (7, 8, 9, 10, 11, 12, 13) hanks in #2010

Size I-9 (5.5mm) crochet hook

Gauge

11 BASE CH/SC = 4" (10cm)

In shell pattern, 2 repeats (SH, sc) and 6 rows = 3" (7.5cm)

In sc finishing, 11 sc = 4" (10cm)

Special Stitches

See Jewel, page 37

YOKE

Make in the same way as Tall Latte V-Neck Yoke (page 52). In order to leave front open, stop before Joining of neck, ending at:

SIZE 33: Row 14—33 shells.

SIZE 36: Row 15—38 shells.

SIZE 39: Row 15—42 shells.

SIZES 42 (45): Row 16—44 shells.

SIZE 48: Row 16—48 shells.

SIZE 51: Row 17—50 shells.

SIZE 54: Row 17—54 shells.

Sizes 39, 48, and 54 require one additional row before joining underarms:

Sizes 39 (48, 54)

Row 16 (17, 18): Ch 3, 2 dc in first dc, *work in pattern to next inc-sh, over inc-sh work (sc in first ch-sp, SH in next ch-sp, sc in next ch-sp)*; repeat from * to * 3 times, work in pattern to end, ending with 3 dc in top of tch, turn. (If making Shannon coat, page 116, mark dc row edges at each end for later.)

JOINING

Join fronts and back with additional sts at underarms. All sizes join in basically the same fashion, except the sizes are at different steps at front neck edges.

Note: After joining underarms, mark the center st of underarm. You don't have to keep moving it up, just keep track of the location of center of side for later.

Size 33

Row 1 (Join): Ch 3, (dc, ch 1, 2 dc) in first sc, *work in pattern to next corner sh, sc in ch-sp of corner sh, ch 1, BASE CH/SC 7 for underarm, sc in ch-sp of next corner sh*; repeat from * to *, work in pattern to end, placing SH in last sc, turn.

Sizes 36 (42, 45, 51)

Row 1: Ch 3, 2 dc in first dc, *work in pattern to next corner sh, sc in ch-sp of corner sh, ch 1, BASE CH/SC 7 (7, 11, 11) for underarm, sc in ch-sp of next corner sh*; repeat from * to *, then work in pattern to end, ending with 3 dc in last sc, turn.
(If making Shannon coat, mark dc row edges at each end for later.)

Sizes 39 (48, 54)

Row 1: Ch 1, sc in first dc, SH in next sc, *work in pattern to next corner sh, sc in ch-sp of corner sh, ch 1, BASE CH/SC 7 (11, 11) for underarm, sc in ch-sp of next corner sh*; repeat from * to *, work in pattern to end, ending with sc in third ch of tch, turn.

Next row fill in pattern at underarms as follows.

Size 33

Row 2: Ch 3, 2 dc in first dc, sc in next ch-sp, *work in pattern, placing SH in sc before underarm, sk next 3 sc, sc in next sc, sk remaining 3 sc of underarm, SH in sc after underarm*; repeat from * to *, work in pattern to end, ending with sc in last ch-sp of sh, 3 dc in top of tch, turn.
(If making Shannon coat, mark dc row edges at each front for later.)

Sizes 36 (42)

Row 2: Ch 1, sc in first dc, repeat Size 33 Row 2 from * to * twice, work in pattern to end, ending with sc in top of tch, turn.

Size 39

Row 2: Ch 3, 2 dc in first sc, repeat Size 33 Row 2 from * to * twice, work in pattern to end, ending with 3 dc in last sc, turn.

Sizes 45 (51)

Row 2: Ch 1, sc in first dc, *work in pattern, placing SH in sc before underarm, sk next 2 sc, sc in next sc, sk next 2 sc, SH in next sc, sk next 2 sc, sc in next sc, sk remaining 2 sc of underarm, SH in next sc*; repeat from * to *, work in pattern to end, ending with sc in top of tch, turn.

Sizes 48 (54)

Row 2: Ch 3, 2 dc in first sc, repeat Size 45 Row 2 from * to * twice, work in pattern to end, ending with 3 dc in last sc, turn.

Stop here for Shannon, continued on page 118.

BODY CONTINUED

Beginning with PATT ROW 1 (2, 1, 2, 2, 1, 2, 1), work even on 22 (24, 26, 28, 30, 32, 34, 36) pattern repeats to approximately 11" (28cm) from underarm, 20 or 21 more rows, ending by working PATT ROW 2 (1, 2, 1, 2, 1, 2, 1) with sc at center of each side at underarm.

Adjusting for length

I place the vents to open just above my pants pockets so I can get into them easily. Shorten or lengthen the body before the side vents by omitting or adding rounds as desired, end by working PATT ROW 2 (1, 2, 1, 2, 1, 2, 1).

SIDE VENTS

There is a sc at center of each side at underarm. Divide body and work each section separately.

First Side Front
Row 1: Beginning as PATT ROW 1 (2, 1, 2, 1, 2, 1, 2), work in pattern on 5½ (6, 6½, 7, 7½, 8, 8½, 9) pattern repeats to sc at center of side at underarm, 3 dc in center sc, turn.
Row 2: Ch 1, sc in first dc, work in pattern, ending as PATT ROW 2 (1, 2, 1, 2, 1, 2, 1), turn.
Row 3: Beginning as PATT ROW 1 (2, 1, 2, 1, 2, 1, 2), work in pattern, ending with 3 dc in last sc, turn.
Repeat Rows 2–3 for 5 times, Row 2 once more, until approximately 7" (18cm) or to desired length, fasten off.

Back

Join with sl st in same sc as last 3 dc of first side Row 1.

Row 1: Ch 3, 2 dc in same sc, work even in pattern on 11 (12, 13, 14, 15, 16, 17, 18) shells to sc at center of side at other underarm, 3 dc in center sc, turn.

Work PATT ROWS 1–2 to same length as First Side Front, fasten off.

Second Side Front

Join with sl st in same sc as last 3 dc of Back Row 1.

Row 1: Ch 3, 2 dc in same sc, work in pattern, end as PATT ROW 1 (2, 1, 2, 1, 2, 1, 2), turn.

Row 2: Begin as PATT ROW 2 (1, 2, 1, 2, 1, 2, 1), work in pattern, end with sc in top of tch, turn.

Repeat Rows 1–2 for 6 times or to same length as First Side Front, fasten off.

SLEEVES

Haru sleeves are short and full-width.

Rnd 1: Same as Jewel Rnd 1 (page 40)—8 (9, 10, 10, 11, 12, 12, 13) pattern repeats.

Work even in established pattern until approximately 4" (10cm) from underarm, for 7 more rounds, fasten off. Make second sleeve in the same way.

Adjusting sleeve length

Feel free to make any length sleeve you please. For half-length, make same as Jewel (page 40), either full-width or tapered. For long, full-width sleeves, simply continue working even rounds to desired length. For long, tapered sleeves, make in the same way as No Sweat (page 45), omitting cuff and working even rounds to desired length.

FINISHING

There is no obvious RS or WS so far. Choose the side you wish to be the public side, now RS of work. Work finishing to gauge 11 sc = 4" (10cm). For Haru finishing, ignore markers at the point of V-neck shaping.

Row 1 (RS): RS facing, join A with sl st in first row edge at lower corner of right-hand front, ch 1, sc in same row edge, make [sc in each sc row edge, 2 sc in each dc row edge] across front and V-neck shaping, sc in each base ch of neck, repeat between [ ] to end, turn.

Row 2 (WS): Ch 1, sc in each sc to end, turn.

Row 3 (RS): Repeat Row 2, fasten off.

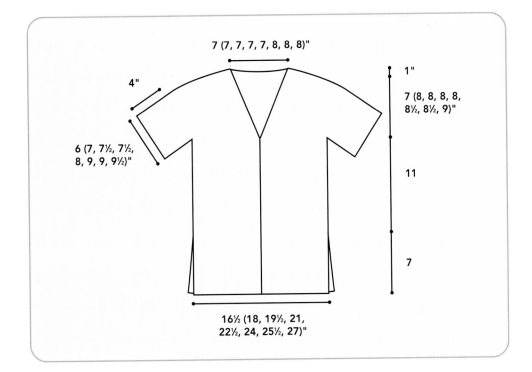

7 (7, 7, 7, 8, 8, 8)"

4"

1"

7 (8, 8, 8, 8, 8½, 8½, 9)"

6 (7, 7½, 7½, 8, 9, 9, 9½)"

11

7

16½ (18, 19½, 21, 22½, 24, 25½, 27)"

SHANNON

Roomy enough for layering, this coat needs your coziest, loftiest yarns. The deep front ribbing turns back for a neck-warming shawl collar. The long coat sleeves are slightly tapered into deeply ribbed cuffs. Wrap and close your coat with the optional Sash-A crocheted belt (page 128), and you're ready for all but the cruelest cold weather.

Yarn Notes: What occasionally happens by accident or mistake, we will now do on purpose. Using medium to heavy worsted weight yarn (ball band symbol 4) and a larger hook, slightly explode the gauge of the previous jacket to make this generously sized coat. The same stitches in a larger gauge cause the coat to be bigger all over, so the translation is not perfect. You'll need to tweak the sleeves and length in order to retain correct proportions, but it does work well.

Size Finder: Choose the size close to your bust measurement plus 4–6" (10–15cm) ease.

SHANNON

Skill Level | EXPERIENCED | 4 MEDIUM

Size

Finished bust: 38 (42, 45, 49, 52, 56, 59)" (96.5 [106.5, 114, 124.5, 132, 142, 150]cm)

Materials

Tahki Shannon; 100% wool; 1¾ oz (50g)/92 yd (84m) (MC)

12 (13, 15, 17, 18, 19, 20) balls in #15

Tahki Torino; 100% extra fine merino wool superwash; 1¾ oz (50g)/94 yd (86m)

4 balls in #122 Fuchsia

Size J-10 (6mm) crochet hook

Gauge

10 BASE CH/SC = 4" (10cm)

In shell pattern, 2 repeats and 6 rows = 3½" (9cm)

In ribbing, 11 sctbl and 11 rows = 4" (10cm), unstretched

Special Stitches

See Jewel, page 37

INSTRUCTIONS

Using the same pattern instructions as Haru (page 112), make an open front V-neck yoke in this slightly larger gauge. To keep things simple, I will refer to the original Haru sizes throughout this larger gauge pattern, but remember: Haru SIZES 33 (36, 39, 42, 45, 48, 51) correspond to Shannon coat SIZES 38 (42, 45, 49, 52, 56, 59).

YOKE AND JOINING

Same as Haru Yoke through underarm Joining Row 2 (page 112), worked as a PATT ROW 2 (1, 2, 1, 1, 2, 1).
Row 3: PATT ROW 1 (2, 1, 2, 2, 1, 2)—22 (24, 26, 28, 30, 32, 34) pattern repeats.

Adjusting for full bust

Matching short rows are worked on each side of fronts. For SIZES 33 (36, 39, 42) there is a sh at center of underarm; for SIZES 45 (48, 51) there is a sc at center of underarm.

First Side Short Rows

Begin as PATT ROW 2 (1, 2, 1, 1, 2, 1), SIZES 33 (36, 39, 42) work in pattern to sh before sh at center of underarm, SIZES 45 (48, 51) work in pattern to second sh before sc at center of underarm, sl st in next ch-sp of sh, turn. SH in next sc, work in pattern to end, end as PATT ROW 1 (2, 1, 2, 2, 1, 2). Put the loop on the hook on hold.

Stitch Pattern

FOR WORKING EVEN

RIB 1 (WS): Ch 1, sctbl in each sc to end, sl st in each of next 2 sc of edge, turn.

RIB 2 (RS): Sk next 2 sl st, sctbl in each sc to end, turn.

FOR INCREASING

RIB 3 (RS): Sk next sl st, sctbl next sl st, sctbl each sc to end, turn—inc 1 sc.

FOR DECREASING

RIB 4 (RS): Sk next 2 sl st, sk next sc, sctbl each remaining sc to end, turn—dec 1 sc.

FOR SHORT ROW
(MAKE 2 ROWS OVER ONE SC OF EDGE)

RIB 5 (WS): Ch 1, sctbl in each sc to end, sl st in next sc of edge, turn.

RIB 6 (RS): Sk next sl st, sctbl each sc to end, turn.

Second Side Short Rows

Same side facing, sk to other underarm, SIZES 33 (36, 39, 42) sk sh at center of underarm, SIZES 45 (48, 51) sk sh past sc at center of underarm. Join new yarn with sl st in next ch-sp of sh, SH in next sc, work in pattern, ending as PATT ROW 2 (1, 2, 1, 1, 2, 1), turn. Begin as PATT ROW 1 (2, 1, 2, 2, 1, 2), work in pattern, end with sl st in ch-sp of last sh, fasten off. Pick up loop on hold, and continue with next row. Note: If you made the bust short rows, when working next row ignore the sl sts of turning, working pattern in sts as facing.

BODY CONTINUED

Beginning with PATT ROW 2 (1, 2, 1, 1, 2, 1), work even on 22 (24, 26, 28, 30, 32, 34) pattern repeats until approximately 8" (20.5cm) from underarm, 10 (11, 10, 10, 10, 11, 11) more rows, end by working PATT ROW 1 (1, 1, 2, 2, 2, 1). Make 2 increases, one to each side of center back.

Hip Shaping: Begin as PATT ROW 2 (2, 2, 1, 1, 1, 2), placing sc (sh, sc, sc, sh, sc, sc) at center of underarm, make next 3 (3, 4, 4, 4, 5, 5) shells in pattern, INC-SH in next sc, make next 3 (3, 3, 4, 4, 4, 5) shells in pattern, INC-SH in next sc, work in pattern to end.

Next Row: Begin as PATT ROW 1 (1, 1, 2, 2, 2, 1), work in pattern to next inc-sh, over inc-sh work (sc in first ch-sp, SH in next ch-sp, sc in next ch-sp), work in pattern to end.

Work even on 24 (26, 28, 30, 32, 34, 36) pattern repeats to approximately 25" (63.5cm) from underarm, 28 (27, 28, 28, 28, 27, 27) more rows or to desired length, fasten off.

SLEEVES

Shannon sleeves are tapered to the wrist, with a deeply ribbed cuff.

Rnd 1: Same as Jewel Rnd 1 (page 40)—8 (9, 10, 10, 11, 12, 12) pattern repeats.

Taper sleeve 1 (2, 3, 3, 3, 4, 4) times over next 24 rounds to approximately 14" (35.5cm) from underarm as follows:

Size 33: PATT RNDS 1–2 for 5 times, PATT RND 1, TAPER 1–5, PATT RND 2, PATT RND 1–2 for 3 times, then PATT RND 1 once more.

Size 36: PATT RNDS 1–2 for 4 times, PATT RND 1, TAPER 1–5 twice, PATT RND 2, PATT RNDS 1–2 for 4 times.

Sizes 39 (42): PATT RNDS 1–2 twice, PATT RND 1, TAPER 1–5 for 3 times, PATT RND 2, PATT RNDS 1–2, then PATT RND 1 once more.

Size 45: PATT RND 2, PATT RNDS 1–2, PATT RND 1, TAPER 1–5 for 3 times, PATT RND 2, PATT RNDS 1–2 twice.

Sizes 48 (51): PATT RND 2, PATT RND 1, TAPER 1–5 for 4 times, PATT RND 2, PATT RND 1.

7 (7, 7, 7, 8, 8, 8) pattern repeats.

Adjusting for length

Shorten or lengthen sleeve before cuff by omitting or adding rounds as desired after tapering is complete. For an open-bottom sleeve, omit the cuffs and work even to desired length.

CUFF

There is no obvious RS or WS until now. All sizes turn, RS now facing. Work sts of cuff to gauge of 11 sts = 4" (10cm).

Rnd 1 (RS): With CC, join with sl st in next dc at or close to underarm, ch 1, sc in same dc, make 4 sc over each pattern repeat by [sc in each dc, sk each ch-sp and sc] around, end with sl st in beg sc, do not turn—28 (28, 28, 28, 32, 32, 32) sc.

Foundation (RS): Ch 1, sc in same sc for first base ch/sc, BASE CH/SC 10, turn—11 sts.

Work RIB 1–2, working even on 11 sc around sleeve, end by working a RIB 1, except end with sl st in last sc of sleeve, fasten off, leaving a few inches of tail for seaming. Hold last row together with foundation, matching sts, whip stitch together through 11 sts, fasten off.

Make second sleeve and cuff in the same way.

FINISHING

Note: Ribbing stretches and molds as needed, but try to keep working gauge to 11 sts and 11 rows = 4" (10cm), not too firm.

RS (as determined by Cuff) now facing, join CC with sl st in first row edge at bottom of right-hand front.

Rnd 1 (RS): Ch 1, sc in same row edge, sc evenly up front to marked dc row edge by [sc in each sc row edge, 2 sc in each dc row edge]; make a corner of 3 sc in marked dc row edge, move marker into center (second sc) of corner; repeat between [ ] across V-neck shaping to base ch of back neck, sc in each neck ch, work down other front same way, do not turn.

COLLAR

From bottom edge to marker at V-neck corner, the ribbing is worked even for front band. Across V-neck shaping, the ribbing stitch count increases by one sc every other row until full collar height. Across back neck, the ribbing row count increases with short rows. From back neck to next marker, ribbing stitch count decreases by one sc every other row until width for front band, then worked even to end.

Note: Don't get too obsessive about row counting, it's not all that critical. Just try to keep the sides of front the same length.

Foundation (RS): Ch 1, sc in same sc for first base ch/sc, BASE CH/SC 7, turn—7 sts.

Work RIB 1–2, working even on 7 sc to V-neck corner, work RIB 1 that ends with the second sl st in sc before corner marker OR in marked sc of corner, depending on your size and length.

Over the next 27 sc of front, increase every other row for Collar as follows:

Work RIB 3, then alternate RIB 1 and 3 for 13 times—21 sc.

Mark the corresponding sc on other side of V-neck shaping, either 27 or 28 from other corner marker.

Begin short rows across back neck:

Work RIB 5–6 even on 21 sc to sc before marker, making 2 rows for every one sc of edge.

Begin decreasing to band width:

Work RIB 1, then alternate RIB 4 and 1 for 13 times, then RIB 4 once more—7 sc.

Work RIB 1–2 even on 7 sc to end, ending with RIB 1, sl st in last sc of edge, fasten off.

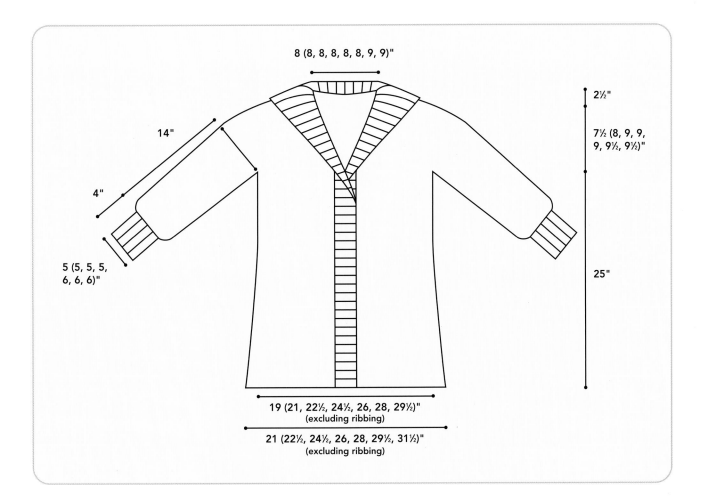

OUTTA SIGHT

Groovy to the max is this mod coat, a slim, duster-length vest. It is built on the same pattern as Insight (page 98), featuring very simple color-blocking and gentle A-line shaping. The front band hugs the back neck and skims down the body, not quite meeting at the bust. Wear it fully open and sweeping the lower calf, or do the optional lacing to pinch the waist.

Yarn Notes: This alpaca blend yarn is fairly lightweight but very warm. If you want a vest to wear indoors, substitute a cooler spring/summer yarn that works close to gauge. Ultra Alpaca is packaged in 100g hanks with a generous amount of yardage. In order to do the color-blocking as shown, you need to purchase the number of hanks stated. However, you won't be using all of it for all the sizes. Here's a guideline for estimating how many it would take if you substitute 50g balls of yarn with approximately 100 yds each:

4 (4, 4, 5, 5, 6, 6) balls in A

2 (2, 3, 3, 3, 4, 4) balls in B, C, D and E

Size Finder: The Fronts do not need to completely cover the bust. Choose the size that is closest to your bust measurement. There is built-in extra room for your hips. However, if your hips are more than 5 inches (12.5cm) larger than your bust, size up. Expect this fabric to grow tremendously in length to given measurements when blocked and hung, so consider carefully before deciding to alter length. Feel free to leave out one color block for below-the-knee length, two blocks for a tunic, or three blocks for a mid-hip length vest.

OUTTA SIGHT

Skill Level	**INTERMEDIATE**

Size

Finished bust: 34 (37, 41, 45, 49, 52, 56)" (86 [94, 104, 114, 124.5, 132, 142]cm)

Materials

Berroco Ultra Alpaca; 50% alpaca, 50% wool; 3½ oz (100g)/215 yd (198m)

2 (2, 2, 3, 3, 3, 3) hanks in #6236 Chianti (A)

1 (1, 2, 2, 2, 2, 2) hanks each in #6227 Henna (B), #6229 Sweet Potato (C), #6230 Mustard (D), #6249 Fennel (E)

Size J-10 (6mm) crochet hook

Gauge

In shell pattern, 2 repeats and 6 rows = 3¾" (9.5cm) (as crocheted), grows to 6 rows = approximately 4¼" (11cm)

10 sc = 4" (10cm)

In cluster pattern of band, 5 repeats (CL, ch 1) = 4" (10cm)

Special Stitches

See Galena, page 91

CL (cluster): Tr3tog in the same st.

Like Insight, this coat begins with a deep U-neck yoke, but it continues straight down the length of the fronts. The same hip shaping as Insight is started higher and repeated down the back for added swing.

YOKE

With A, make in the same way as Insight (page 100) up to Body, through joining at underarms and bust short rows and ending with:

All Sizes
Next Row: Work in PATT ROW 1 even on 15 (17, 19, 21, 23, 24, 25) pattern repeats, fasten off A.

BODY

Continue to work front edges even. AT THE SAME TIME, begin color block sequence: Over 48 rows, work 12 rows each in [B, C, D, E].

Adjusting for length

To maintain even color blocks, shorten or lengthen coat by adjusting the same number of rows in each color. For Petite or a shorter coat, work 44 rows, with 11 rows done in each color (3" [7.5cm] shorter). For Tall or a longer coat, work 52 rows, with 13 rows in each color (3" [7.5cm] longer).

BODY CONTINUED

Join B, work body even on 15 (17, 19, 21, 23, 24, 25) pattern repeats for 2 (2, 3, 3, 3, 3, 3) rows, end by working PATT ROW 1 (1, 2, 2, 2, 2, 2).

Note: Mark center dc of each inc-sh and move or wrap markers up as you go.

Hip Shaping 1: Begin as PATT ROW 2 (2, 1, 1, 1, 1, 1), work next 5 (6, 7, 8, 9, 9, 10) shells in pattern, INC-SH in next sc, work 2 (2, 3, 3, 3, 4, 4) shells in pattern, INC-SH in next sc, work in pattern to end, turn.

Hip Shaping 2: Begin as PATT ROW 1 (1, 2, 2, 2, 2), *work in pattern to next inc-sh, over inc-sh work (sc in second dc, SH in third dc, sc in 4th dc)*; repeat from * to *, work in pattern to end, turn—17 (19, 23, 25, 26, 28) pattern repeats.

Work even in pattern for 11 (11, 11, 7, 7, 7, 7) rows, ending with 1 sc at each marker.

Hip Shaping 3: *Work in pattern to next marked sc, INC-SH in marked sc*; repeat from * to *, work in pattern to end, turn.

Hip Shaping 4: *Work in pattern to next inc-sh, over inc-sh work (sc in second dc, SH in third dc, sc in fourth dc)*; repeat from * to *, work in pattern to end, turn. Repeat last 13 (13, 13, 9, 9, 9, 9) rows for 1 (1, 1, 2, 2, 2, 2) times, work even in pattern to end of color sequence of 48 rows, change to A in last st, fasten off E—21 (23, 25, 29, 31, 32, 34) pattern repeats.

FINISHING

BAND

There is no obvious RS or WS until you make that determination now. Do not turn, RS now facing, rotate and work Band around front and neck edges. Band is crocheted to gauge 10 st = 4" (10cm) and should neither pull in nor stretch out the front edges.

Rnd 1 (RS): With A, ch 1, [2 sc in each dc row edge, sc in each sc row edge], sc in each base ch of back neck, repeat between [ ] to bottom, turn—there will be an odd number of sc, exact number not critical.

Rnd 2 (WS): Ch 1, sc in each sc to end, turn.

Rnd 3: Ch 4, tr in first sc, [ch 1, sk next sc, CL in next sc] to end, except omit last CL, instead end tr2tog in last sc, turn.

Rnd 4: Ch 1, sc in first cl, 2 sc in each ch-1 sp around, ending with sc in top of tch, turn.

Rnd 5: Ch 1, sc in each sc to end, fasten off.

ARMHOLES

With A, finish armholes with scallop edging in the same way as Galena (page 93).

LACING

With A, ch 200 (approximately 60" [152.5cm]), sl st in second ch from hook, sl st in each ch to end, fasten off, weave ends. Loosely lace like a shoelace using corresponding holes on either side of front band, from waist to just under the bust as shown in photo.

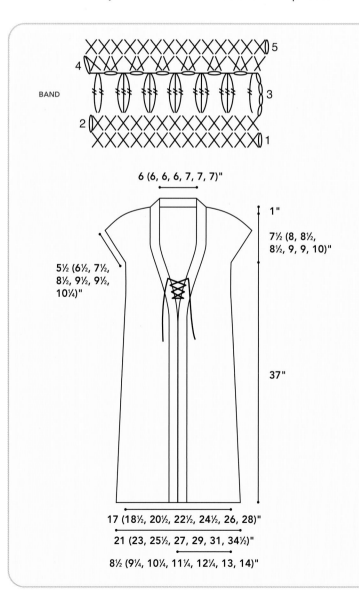

|7|
ADDED INTEREST
BELTS AND CLOSURES

There are no buttonholes or loops in my sweaters, so you can leave your options open. Once you crochet some holes and sew on the buttons, you are stuck with them. By using the following belts and button links instead, you can swap out closures whenever the mood strikes.

The most basic crochet stitches are used to make the array of belts. You can simply tie the ends of the belt (Sash-A, page 128) or purchase a hardware buckle (Hardware, page 130), crochet a tab and button closure (Software, page 132), or make a belt that combines methods (Multitask, page 134).

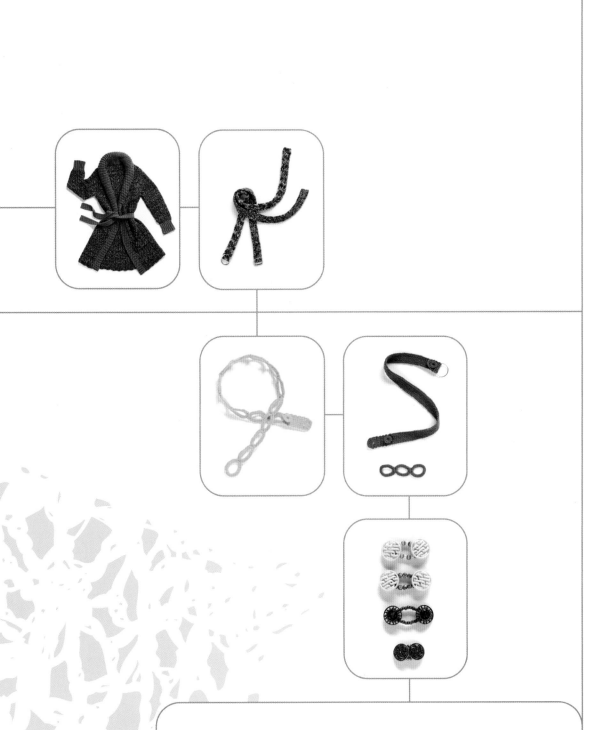

YARN NOTES

You can create a functional, decorative belt in just about any yarn and any fiber, and as long or wide as desired. The most useful yarn weight for a belt is worsted (ball band symbol 4) or heavier. Finer yarns may not have enough body. If you want to use a finer yarn, hold two or even three strands together to crochet.

Skill Level	BEGINNER	[4 MEDIUM]

Size
Adjust to fit

Materials
Tahki Torino; 100% extrafine merino wool superwash; 1¾ oz (50g)/94 yd (85m)

2 balls in #122 Fuchsia; more yarn required for longer or wider belt

Size I-9 (5.5mm) crochet hook

Gauge
14 sl st = 4" (10cm)

Special Stitches
This sl st pattern, made lengthwise, is good for belts that need a bit of stretch and give. Once you've turned at the end a row and start working back across, you will find that the previous rows of sl sts lie really flat to the back of the work. You want to insert the hook into the loop that lies at the very top edge. Technically that is the front loop only of each sl st, but the clearest way to see what loop to use is to call it the top loop.

SASH-A

This is the belt that wraps and ties around the Shannon coat (page 116).

INSTRUCTIONS

Note: The tendency is to make slip stitches tighter and tighter each row. Try to keep your gauge the same as the foundation chain throughout.

Ch 210 to measure approximately 60" (152.5cm) stretched.

Row 1: Sl st in second ch from hook by inserting hook in top lp only of ch, sl st in top lp of each remaining ch, turn.

Row 2: Ch 1, sl st in top lp only of each sl st to end, turn.
Repeat ROW 2 for 10 more rows, or to desired width of belt, fasten off.

Skill Level	BEGINNER	6 SUPER BULKY

Size

Adjust to fit

Materials

Lion Brand Fettuccini; 45% wool, 45% acrylic, 10% nylon; 1¾ oz (50g)/33 yd (30m)

One ball in #207 Camouflage, more yarn required for longer or wider belt

Size M or N (9mm) crochet hook

Purchased belt buckle, 2" (5cm) wide

Gauge

8 sl st = 4" (10cm)

Pattern Note

For less bulk, try this belt in a chunky weight yarn as shown in blue above, using one ball Caron Black Magic (50% wool, 50% acrylic; 1¾ oz [50g]/59 yd [54m]) in #0003 Violet Sky and a size K-10½ (6.5mm) crochet hook, and at a gauge of 11 sl st = 4" (10cm).

Instructions: Ch 120 to measure approximately 42" (106.5cm) slightly stretched. Make same as in pattern, repeating ROW 2 for 5 more times, or to desired width. Finish in the same way.

HARDWARE

This sample is narrow and bold, crocheted in super-bulky yarn, with a purchased belt buckle.

INSTRUCTIONS

Ch 80 to measure approximately 40" (101.5cm) slightly stretched.

Row 1–2: Make same way as Sash-A Rows 1–2 (page 129). Repeat Row 2 for 2 more times, fasten off, leaving several inches of tail for sewing.

FINISHING

This belt is a bit thick for folding over on itself, so I chose to whip stitch the belt edge directly onto the buckle. Thread tail on a yarn needle, and sew narrow end of belt to the center post of buckle, wrapping the yarn to cover the post and sewing securely through the belt fabric several times. Fasten off, and weave ends.

SOFTWARE

This easy-to-crochet and highly adaptable belt is made of links that are joined as you go and uses very little yarn. Create the perfect length to wear high around your waist, low and hip-slung, or anywhere you please by making fewer or more links. Close the belt with a clever tab that can be buttoned around any link to adjust the belt length.

Yarn Notes: I prefer to use a sturdy, smooth, worsted weight yarn for the links. The stitches have to slide around the chain stitch ring to be distributed evenly, and that means a bit of manhandling. The heavier the yarn, the bolder the links. However, you can certainly use any yarn or combination of yarns held together to make any size links you please.

Skill Level   EASY   [4 MEDIUM]

Size
Adjust to fit

Materials
Morehouse Merino 3-Strand worsted weight; 100% merino wool; 2 oz (56g)/140 yd (128m)

1 hank in Sunflower (sample required approx 1 oz, one Link requires approx 3 yards [2.7m])

Size H-8 (5mm) crochet hook

Size F-5 (3.75mm) crochet hook for button only

One ½" (13mm) diameter plastic bone ring for button

Gauge
Crocheted firmly, 20 sc = 4" (10cm) (stitches will be further compressed around ring). One link as joined stretches into an oval 2¼" long x 1¼" wide (5.5 x 3cm). Tab is 3" long x 1¼" wide (7.5 x 3cm); Button is ¾" (20mm) in diameter.

INSTRUCTIONS

LINKS

Belt is made of links, each one joined to 4 sts of the previous link as you go, working firmly.

First Link (RS): Ch 16, sl st in beg ch to form a ring, ch 1, 32 sc in ring, sliding stitches close together as you go to distribute evenly around ring, sl st in beg sc, fasten off, leaving long tail.

Second Link: Ch 16, sl st in beg ch to form a ring, ch 1, 13 sc in ring. Hold end to end with previous Link, RS facing, locate beg sc of previous Link (where sl st closed). Sl st to join by: *Insert hook from front to back into top of beg sc of previous Link, make sl st, sc in ring*; repeat from * to * 3 times, 15 sc in ring, sl st in beg sc, fasten off. Distribute stitches evenly around ring.

Make and join additional Links in the same way as second Link until desired length. Weave in ends.

TAB

Row 1: Hold last Link made with RS facing, locate beg sc, sk beg sc, sk back next 4 sc, join with sl st in next sc, ch 1, sc in same sc, sc in next 5 sc, turn—6 sc.

Row 2–10: Ch 1, sc in 6 sc, turn.

Row 11: Ch 1, sc in each of first 2 sc, ch 3, sk next 2 sc, sc in each of last 2 sc, turn.

Row 12: Ch 1, sc in each of first 2 sc, 2 sc in ch-sp, sc in each of last 2 sc, turn.

Row 13: Ch 1, sc2tog first 2 sc, sc in each of next 2 sc, sc2tog last 2 sc, turn—4 sc.

Row 14: Ch 1, sc in 4 sc, fasten off.

BUTTON

Rnd 1: Using smaller hook, leaving a few inches of tail, ch 2, make 6 sc in second ch from hook, sl st in beg sc, pull beg tail through center of ring and keep on RS of work.

Rnd 2: Ch 1, hold bone ring in back of Rnd 1, inserting hook into sc of Rnd 1 and into center of bone ring each time, 3 sc in each sc around, sl st in beg sc, fasten off, leaving a few inches of tail.

Thread ending tail on yarn needle, sew tail into center of Button to meet beg tail, knot tails together securely on RS. The WS of Button is the public side. Using tails, sew Button to RS of Tab, close to end of last Link. Weave ends. To close belt, wrap belt around body, slip buttonhole end of Tab through any Link at other end of belt from back to front, fold Tab to front so buttonhole meets Button.

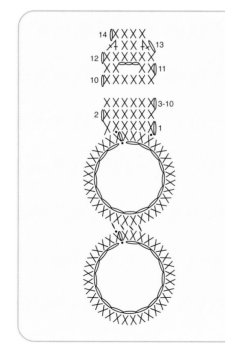

MULTITASK

A hybrid belt, combining the solid slip stitch fabric from Hardware with a tab closure like Software. For maximum flexibility, to easily switch from waist to hip-slung, put tabs at both ends of the belt. Then you can swap out the connector between tabs to change the length of the belt.

Skill Level	EASY	**4** MEDIUM

Size
Adjust to fit

Materials
Morehouse Merino 3-Strand worsted weight; 100% Merino Wool; 2 oz (56g)/140 yd (128m)

1 hank in Pacific (teal), more yarn needed for longer or wider belt

Size I-9 (5.5mm) crochet hook

Size H-8 (5mm) crochet hook

Size F-5 (3.75mm) crochet hook for button

Two ½" (13mm) diameter plastic bone rings for buttons or purchased ¾" (20mm) buttons

2" (5cm) diameter brass craft or macramé ring (optional)

Gauge
In sl st of belt body, using I-9 (5.5 mm) hook, 14 sl st = 4" (10cm)

In sc of tab, using H-8 (5 mm) hook, crocheted firmly, 20 sc = 4" (10cm)

INSTRUCTIONS

BELT BODY
Ch 110 to measure approximately 30" (76cm), make in the same way as Sash-A (page 129) with 9 sl st rows. Do not fasten off.

TABS
Turn, make first tab across short end of belt body.
Row 1: Ch 1, make 6 sc evenly spaced across edge, turn.
Row 2–14: Same as Software Tab Rows 2–14 (page 132). On other end of belt body, join with sl st in first row edge, make same way as first tab.

LINKS
Make same way as Software Link for 3 joined links, or as many as needed.

BUTTONS
Make 2 buttons in the same way as Software Button.

FINISHING
Position and sew a button on each tab in the same way as Software. Use the separate set of links or craft ring between the tabs to adjust belt length as desired.
Note: If you discover your belt is too long, you can adjust by moving the buttons up onto the belt body on either or both sides.

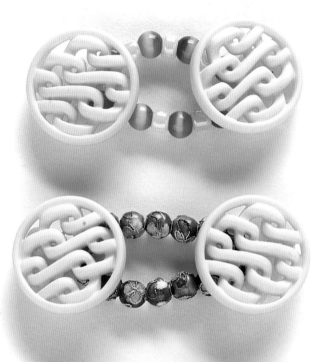

Skill Level	EASY (NO CROCHET REQUIRED)	6 SUPER BULKY

Materials

BUTTONS: Shank buttons with a loop at the back work best. Make sure they are small enough to go through the hole, but large enough to stay in the hole, generally from ¾" (20mm) to 1" (2.5cm) diameter.

BEADS: Use any small beads that won't slide through the shank, generally 3–6mm, like E-beads, small pony beads, 4–6mm round pearls, or pebble beads.

STRING: My favorite material to use is elastic cord trademarked as Stretch Magic, but other brands, available at craft stores in the jewelry-making section, usually used for stringing bracelets and necklaces, are fine. The stretch makes it easier to use: You can usually poke the end right through the bead, and the knot really holds. It comes in different diameters and colors. I prefer the 1mm clear. But it is possible to string the links on anything you have around, including the yarn from the garment, some sturdy thread or string, or even fine wire if you are handy with pliers.

FOR EACH SET OF LINKS

Two matching (or not!) shank buttons

Beads, a dozen or so, depending on size of beads and distance needed to link

Stretch Magic or similar cord (1mm clear), a few inches

IN-LINE LINKS

The way my garments drape, the front bands on the cardigans and vests are often not stiff or sturdy enough for sewing on buttons. For those wimpy edges, instead of creating the usual buttonholes or button loops, I use the holes already available in the front bands as buttonholes and close with these links, like cufflinks. Make as many sets as you want and use different sets as the mood strikes.

INSTRUCTIONS

Lay out the garment, having the front bands meet where you want to use a link, and position the buttons on either side to make sure there are holes available and also to check the fit of the buttons. Measure the distance between the button shanks; that's the distance apart you have to string them.

Slip one end of the cord through the button shank, slide the button to center of cord, string enough beads on either side of the button to equal the distance needed, slip one end of the cord through the shank of the second button (if buttons have a one-way design, see that they match, if desired), securely tie the ends with an overhand knot, pull tight, trim ends.

How simple is that?

glossary

BASE CH/SC (base chain single crochet): I am an enthusiastic supporter of this technique. No more too-tight base chains that choke up or too-loose ones that sag. This method creates a foundation chain and row of sc at the same time; is easy, sturdy, and elastic; and makes quite an elegant solution, especially for necklines.

BASE CH/SC AS A FLAT FOUNDATION

FIRST STITCH: Ch 2, insert hook into the second ch from hook (into the front face of the chain *and* under the nub at the back of the chain) under 2 lps. YO and draw up a lp. There are 2 lps on hook. YO and draw through 2 lps on hook.

SECOND STITCH: Insert hook under 2 strands at the forward edge of the stem of the previous sc. It will resemble the way you insert the hook into a chain. YO and draw up a lp. There are 2 lps on hook. YO and draw through one lp on hook. You have just made the "chain" that lies along the base of the foundation. There are 2 lps on hook. YO and draw through 2 lps on hook. You have just made the "sc."

THIRD STITCH: Insert hook into the "chain" at the base of the stitch just made, into the front face *and* under the back nub, under 2 strands. YO and draw up a lp. There are 2 lps on hook. YO and draw through one lp on hook. You have just made the "chain." YO and draw through 2 lps on hook. You have just made the "sc." Make the remaining base ch/sc same as third stitch, except the last stitch.

LAST STITCH: Insert hook into the "chain," under 2 strands. YO and draw up a lp, YO and draw through 2 lps on hook.

Note: Notice the 1st and last base ch/sc stitches are missing a step and thus are a bit shorter than the others. I like to compress the ends of this foundation. It keeps the ends neater when work your first row of stitches.

The BASE CH/SC is also useful for adding stitches at the end of a row or when joining the underarm of a seamless garment. You can make a BASE CH/SC after completing *any* stitch. The stitch just made before the base ch/sc will always have 2 lps at the top of the stitch, the ones you would normally work under. Just below that, there are strands that form the "stem." Whatever the stitch, you will begin the BASE CH/SC by inserting the hook under 2 strands of the forward edge of the stem of the stitch just made, closest to the top lps of the stitch. I always call for a "ch 1" to begin, so as not to compress the end.

I used a type of crochet shorthand in this book that requires you to be responsible for becoming familiar with the stitch pattern as you go. It's not difficult; you do it automatically anyway.

WORK IN PATTERN: "Work in pattern to next whatever" means continue to work across in the stitch pattern as established, stopping in the logical place right before the whatever.

WORK EVEN: Work pattern rows or rounds as established, without increasing or decreasing. "Work even for a million-thousand rows" means keep going for a million-thousand more rows on the same number of pattern repeats.

BASE CH/SC

STEP 1:

ch 2, insert hook in 2nd ch from hook.

STEP 2:

YO, draw yarn through st.

STEP 3:

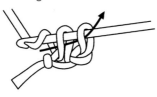

YO, draw yarn through 2 lps on hook.

STEP 4:

First sc made. Insert hook under 2 strands at the forward edge of previous sc.

STEP 5:

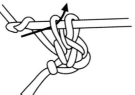

YO, draw up a lp (2 lps on hook), YO, draw through 1 lp on hook for ch.

STEP 6:

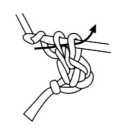

Ch made (2 lps on hook). YO, draw through 2 lps on hook.

STEP 7:

Second sc made. Insert hook under the first 2 strands of the ch at the base of last sc.

STEP 8:

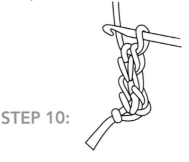

YO, draw up a lp (2 lps on hook), YO, draw through 1 lp on hook for ch.

STEP 9:

Ch made (2 lps on hook). YO, draw through 2 lps on hook.

STEP 10:

Third sc made.

Repeat steps 7–10 for desired length of foundation chain.

abbreviations & symbols

Crochet skill level symbols and ball band symbols for yarn weight are the standardized systems created by the Craft Yarn Council of America. See and download a complete handbook of yarn standards and guidelines from the CYCA-sponsored website, www.yarnstandards.com.

Abbreviations for special stitches or stitch combinations are explained in each pattern.

SPECIAL STITCHES

= examples of shells (SH)

= V-st

= examples of clusters (CL)

= picot

STITCH KEY

• = slip stitch (sl st)

⬯ = chain (ch)

X = single crochet (sc)

T = half double crochet (hdc)

= double crochet (dc)

= treble crochet (tr)

ABBREVIATIONS

beg	begin, beginning		rnd(s)	round, rounds
bp	back post		RS	right side
ch	chain, chain stitch		sc	single crochet
ch-	refers to a chain or space previously made		sc2tog	single crochet two together
ch-sp	chain space		sh	shell
cl	cluster		sk	skip
dc	double crochet		sl st	slip stitch
dc2tog	double crochet two stitches together		sp(s)	space, spaces
dec	decrease, decreases, decreasing		st(s)	stitch, stitches
dtr	double triple crochet		tch	turning chain
foll	follow, follows, following		tbl	through back loop
fp	front post		tog	together
hdc	half double crochet		tr	triple or treble crochet
inc	increase, increases, increasing		WS	wrong side
lp(s)	loop, loops		yo	yarn over
patt	pattern, patterns			

the yarns

The yarns featured in the book should be widely available; however, if you cannot find them you can contact the yarn companies below or visit the websites for information, or substitute yarn of the same weight.

BERROCO
PO Box 367
Uxbridge, MA 01569
www.berroco.com

BROWN SHEEP COMPANY
100662 County Road 16
Mitchell, NE 69357
800-826-9136
www.brownsheep.com

CARON INTERNATIONAL
Customer Service
PO Box 222
Washington, NC 27889
800-868-9194
www.caron.com
www.shopcaron.com

CLASSIC ELITE YARNS
122 Western Avenue
Lowell, MA 01851
www.classiceliteyarns.com

COATS & CLARK
Consumer Services
Po Box 12229
Greenville, SC 29612
800-648-1479
www.coatsandclark.com

DMC CORP
South Hackensack Avenue
Port Kearny Building 10F
South Kearny, NJ 07032
973-589-0606 X3046
www.dmc-Usa.com

LANA GROSSA YARNS
Distributed by Unicorn Books and Crafts, Inc.
www.unicornbooks.com

LILY CHIN SIGNATURE COLLECTION
Distributed by A2Z Fibers
267-523-1100
www.lilychinsignaturecollection.com

LION BRAND YARNS
135 Kero Road
Carlstadt, NJ 07072
800-258-9276
www.lionbrand.com

MOREHOUSE FARM MERINO
Milan, NY 12571
866-470-4852
www.morehousefarm.com

NORO YARN
Distributed by Kfi
www.knittingfever.com

PLYMOUTH YARN
PO Box 28
Bristol, PA 19007
www.plymouthyarn.com

SOUTH WEST TRADING COMPANY
918 S. Park Lane Suite 102
Tempe, AZ 85281
866-794-1818
www.soysilk.com

TAHKI STACY CHARLES, INC.
Distributor of Tahki, S. Charles and Filatura Di Crosa Yarns
70-30 80Th Street, Building #36
Ridgewood, NY 11385
800-338-YARN
www.tahkistacycharles.com

VERMONT ORGANIC FIBERS (O-WOOL)
52 Seymour St, Suite 8
Middlebury, VT 05753
802-388-4351
www.vtorganicfiber.com

resources

FOR MORE CROCHET STITCHES PATTERNS AND HOW-TOS:

Harmony Guides, *300 Crochet Stitches,* Vol. 6, Collins & Brown Ltd., London, 1998.

Harmony Guides, *200 More Crochet Stitches,* Vol. 7, Collins & Brown Ltd., London, 1998.

Encyclopedia of Crochet, Donna Kooler, Leisure Arts, 2002.

The Crochet Stitch Bible, Betty Barnden, Krause Publications, 2004.

Crocheting for Dummies, Karen Manthey and Susan Brittain, Wiley Publishing Inc., 2004.

A SUPERB TEXT FOR SIZING KNITWEAR, APPLICABLE TO CROCHET:

A Knitter's Template: Easy Steps to Great-Fitting Garments, Laura Militzer Bryant and Barry Klein, Martingale & Company, 2002.

A WITTY, COOL BOOK OF KNITWEAR FOR LARGER SIZES:

Big Girl Knits, Jillian Moreno and Amy R. Singer, Potter Craft, 2006.

FOR TIPS ON WARDROBE STYLING AND FIT FOR WOMEN OF ALL SIZES:

What Not to Wear, Trinny Woodall and Susannah Constantine, Riverhead Books, 2002.

Figure It Out: The Real Woman's Guide to Great Style, Geri Brin and Tish Jett with Joanna Goddard, Sixth & Spring Books, 2004.

Color Me Confident: Change Your Look, Change Your Life!, Veronique Henderson and Pat Henshaw, Hamlyn, 2006.

Figure Magazine: The New Shape of Fashion, Soho Publishing.

LINKS

CROCHET GUILD OF AMERICA
1100-H Brandywine Blvd.
Zanesville, OH 43702-7303
www.crochet.org

CRAFT YARN COUNCIL OF AMERICA
www.craftyarncouncil.com